IBN ʿARABĪ

THE VOYAGE OF NO RETURN

Other Books on Ibn ʿArabī
Available From The Islamic Texts Society

Quest for the Red Sulphur
Seal of the Saints
Sufi Metaphysics and Qur'ānic Prophets

MUSLIM PERSONALITIES SERIES

IBN ʿARABĪ
THE VOYAGE OF NO RETURN

CLAUDE ADDAS

Translated from the French
by David Streight

THE ISLAMIC TEXTS SOCIETY

translated from the French by David Streight

First published as *Ibn ʿArabī et le voyage sans retour*,
Édition du Seuil 1996

This edition published in 2000 by
The Islamic Texts Society
Miller's House
Kings Mill Lane
Great Shelford
Cambridge CB22 5EN, U.K.

Reprint 2010

British Library Cataloguing-in-Publication Data.
A catalogue record for this book is
available from the British Library.

ISBN 978 0946621 74 3 paper

Contents

Should Ibn ʿArabī Be Burned?

EVEN IF SALĪM I did dabble in poetry, he was certainly not a dreamer. Master of the Ottoman empire—having casually scattered the bodies of his relatives along the way—the father of Sulaymān the Magnificent was a conqueror in a hurry. On 28 September 1516, he entered Damascus; Syria was his. Egypt was next in line. On 7 February 1517, after bitter struggles with the Mamluks, he arrived victorious in Cairo. Back in Damascus by the beginning of October, Salīm immediately began the construction of a mosque and a mausoleum that would from then on harbour the tomb of Ibn ʿArabī. He had piously visited the tomb during his previous stay in the city, at a time when preparations for his expedition to Egypt would normally have garnered his full attention. The tomb lay behind a fence, abandoned among the weeds. Salīm personally oversaw the construction project, which progressed quickly. On 5 February 1518, Friday prayer was celebrated there for the first time in the Sultan's presence.

The personage so royally honoured was not someone who, at the time, was much on the minds of the Damascene dignitaries. A few years earlier, and only after considerable effort, a Moroccan traveller was able to locate the private cemetery of the Banū Zakī where Ibn ʿArabī's remains lay. At the time, Ibn ʿArabī's work was the target of violent polemics in Syria, and he himself, labelled as anathemous, was remembered only because of posthumous hatred that his name still evoked. There is thus good reason to wonder about the fervent attention paid by Salīm to a spiritual master whose teachings were considered as obscure as they were abhorrent. After all, Salīm was not a metaphysician, nor did he have anything to gain politically from his actions. Granted, there was a text (quite apocryphal) attributed to Ibn ʿArabī that supposedly predicted, in sibylline terms, the great destiny of the Ottoman dynasty and, in particular, the conquest of Syria. But this fabrication was clearly composed *post eventum*, and it is most improbable that Salīm had ever heard of it. Thus, the sultan's unexpected devotion—a devotion that was to be imitated by the majority of his successors—remains unexplained.

Was it a matter of justice whose time had come? Three centuries earlier, Muḥammad b. ʿAlī al-ʿArabī al-Ḥātimī al-Ṭa'ī, called 'Muḥyī al-dīn' ('the Vivifier of Religion'), arrived in Damascus from his native Andalusia and was welcomed in a manner befitting an eminent Sufi. At the end of his many travels, he had made a conscious decision to take up residence in the Syrian capital. And it was there that, in great peace and surrounded by those who venerated him, he passed away on 8 November 1240 (630 AH) at the age of seventy-eight lunar years. Just as peacefully, his body was transported to what would be its final resting place on Mount Qāsiyūn. Of worldly goods, he had left absolutely nothing to those who mourned him that day, for, as an adolescent, he had given up all possessions. And yet, the literary corpus that he bequeathed was of colossal proportion.

Whether he be considered a philosopher or a mystic, a

heretic or a saint, one fact remains irrefutable: with over four hundred works to his name, Ibn ʿArabī is among the most prolific writers of Arabic literature. If some of his works are short, there are others that are thousands of pages long. The *Dīwān al-maʿārif* (*The Collection of Divine Knowledge*), for example, is a collection of poetry which Ibn ʿArabī compiled towards the end of his life with a view of including in it all of his poems; it contains tens of thousands. of verses. Similarly, there is his commentary on the Qur'ān in sixty-four volumes, never completed and now lost. And, above all, there are the thirty-seven volumes of the *Futūḥāt al-makkiyya*, the *Meccan Illuminations*.

The first draft of the *Futūḥāt* was completed in December 1231. Ibn ʿArabī bequeathed it to his son, "and after him, to his descendants and to all Muslims in the West and in the East, on land and on sea".[1] What this means is that Ibn ʿArabī never intended this summation of his ideas to be used only by a handful of scholars. His message was addressed to Muslims everywhere and for all time to come. After a vision he experienced in his youth, Ibn ʿArabī declared, "I then knew that my word would reach the two horizons, that of the West and that of the East." Has history proven him right? When one considers that for seven centuries his work has never stopped being read, meditated and commented upon in all of Islam's vernacular languages —attacked also, but we will return to this subject later; when one knows the tremendous influence that it has had on all of Sufism ('the mystical dimension of Islam,' to use Annemarie Schimmel's expression)—on both the erudite and popular expressions of Sufism—one is forced to respond affirmatively. Were it otherwise, the *ʿulamā*''s con-

[1] *Futūḥāt al-makkiyya* (hereafter *Fut.*), Cairo, 1329 AH, IV, p. 554.

demnation of Ibn ʿArabī would have ceased long ago. The fact that they have been battling him continuously since the end of the thirteenth century is because they know, beyond a shadow of a doubt, that the enemy they pursue remains unvanquished and that, overtly or covertly, his work continues to be a major reference for the 'Men of the Path'.

There are a number of historical, political, and socio-cultural factors that we cannot deal with here but which have contributed to the proliferation of Ibn ʿArabī's ideas; a proliferation that polemics have been powerless to stop. Undoubtedly, this has partly been due to the exhaustive nature of the teachings outlined in the *Futūḥāt*: ontology, cosmology, hagiology, prophetology, eschatology, exegesis, jurisprudence, ritual, and so on. There is no question which does not find an answer—if not a number of answers—in this compendium of spiritual sciences. The *Doctor Maximus* was always concerned, when dealing with particularly difficult questions, with pointing out the variety of opinions available. He excluded none of the interpretations that were proffered, although in each case he would point out his preference. Nevertheless, and contrary to an opinion that has recently been circulating that he was a *ẓāhirite*,[2] Ibn ʿArabī was attached to no juridical or theological school. He was an independent thinker in the strongest sense of the term. This is not to say that he rejected the legacy of the masters who preceded him. On the contrary, he was in complete solidarity with them. Whatever his adversaries may say, Ibn ʿArabī was not an 'innovator', at least not in the pejorative sense that they give the word. The *Futūḥāt* are first and foremost the expression of an

[2] *Ẓāhirism*: the name of a school of law that recognizes only the literal (*ẓāhir*) text of the Qur'ān and the sayings of the Prophet as legal sources.

extraordinary synthesis that gathers together and puts into order the *membra disjecta* of a long and rich mystical tradition. In some cases, this material had never previously been published. Though occasionally bordering on the audacious, the ideas that appear in the *Futūḥāt* were present, in one way or another, well before its author came into the world.

The second draft of the *Futūḥāt*—of which the original manuscript is extent—was completed in 1238, two years before Ibn ʿArabī's death. It contains a complete and definitive statement of his teachings. One can observe straightaway that the major ideas developed in the work and the vocabulary used to express them had already appeared in the writings of his youth. Moreover, Ibn ʿArabī incorporated a certain number of short treatises into the *Futūḥāt*, with practically no modification whatsoever. It would thus be useless to attempt to fit the evolution of his thought to the stages of his life. What is being dealt with here is a homogeneous development of a doctrine that is based on unchanging and unchangeable premises. And if at some point or other the earliest writings are less explicit than those that came later, this in no way means that Ibn ʿArabī did not already have a sufficiently clear view of the subject at hand. The political situation in the West, where his writing career began, necessitated a certain reserve on his part. Protected by powerful individuals and surrounded by a circle of faithful disciples, Ibn ʿArabī was able to write more freely when he reached the East. There again, however, he continued to take precautions. The circulation of a number of his works was limited while he was still alive.

In fact, it was from about the end of the thirteenth century, when this practice of secrecy was no longer observed, that the polemics destined to be waged, even up to the present day, began. The circulation of the *Fuṣūṣ al-ḥikam* (*The Bezels of Wisdom*), and the numerous commentaries written by the first three generations of Ibn ʿArabī's disciples, played a considerable role in this regard. The *Fuṣūṣ al-ḥikam*, which is much more concise than the *Futūḥāt* and which distils the essential metaphysical and hagiographical teachings of Ibn ʿArabī into about a hundred pages, was more open to attack by malevolent readers. As devoted as they were to their master, Ibn ʿArabī's disciples used vocabulary that was much more philosophical, and thus more 'suspect', in their commentaries. In so doing, they helped to make the *Fuṣūṣ* the target of choice for his adversaries.

An Ever-renewed Trial

It would be difficult for someone to imagine a member of parliament today demanding a stop to the circulation of Meister Eckhart's works on the basis of John XXII's papal bull *In Agro Dominico*. In 1979, in Egypt, a member of parliament managed to get the Assembly of the People to withdraw the *Futūḥāt* from the market. Fortunately, the measure was subsequently abrogated; and yet the case is indicative of the problems that writings nearly eight centuries old continue to present to the Muslim consciousness. Revered by some as the Shaykh al-Akbar, 'the greatest of masters', and cursed by others, who considered him to be an enemy of the true faith, no one is indifferent to Ibn ʿArabī.

The first skirmishes broke out in the second half of the thirteenth century. In reality, they were little more than potshots, and quite inconsequential. The systematic attacks against Ibn ʿArabī and his school did not get into full swing until the early part of the fourteenth century, when a doctor of the Law (*faqīh*) by the name of Ibn Taymiyya (d. 1328) set about attempting to demonstrate the heretical nature of his teachings. Ibn Taymiyya was almost as prolific as Ibn ʿArabī; he indefatigably composed numerous 'legal opinions' (*fatāwā*) which, in the Saudi Arabia edition, fill thirty-seven volumes. Relying on quotations from scripture, he denounced the theses that he found in Ibn ʿArabī's writing. It must be admitted that he had a solid grasp of the works he was refuting. His critiques were primarily aimed against the *Fuṣūṣ*, although he was also clearly familiar with the *Futūḥāt*, which he appears to have found helpful. We shall spare the reader the long list of Ibn Taymiyya's charges, but their number gives testimony, in both space and time, to polemics whose persistence astounds the Western observer. Ibn Taymiyya had a number of imitators, although not all of them had his scruples. It is interesting to point out that, when the famous Ibn Khaldūn was invited to judge a controversy that had arisen in Alexandria, he delivered a judicial sentence that ordained the burning of Ibn ʿArabī's books.

The extent of this literature against Ibn ʿArabī should not, however, overly disturb us. Clearly, the judgements hostile to the Shaykh al-Akbar are manifold, but their content remains unchanged. With very few exceptions, they were the same arguments, proffered by Ibn Taymiyya, that have been used over and over again, and they refer to the same texts that he had dealt with. Moreover, the malevolence of their language—'*rhetoric oblige*'—often masked a judgement that was much more subtle than first appears. Dhahabī (d. 1348), one of Ibn Taymiyya's students, frequently stated his opposition to Ibn ʿArabī, and yet it was he who wrote that, "As far as I am concerned, this man [that is, Ibn ʿArabī] may have been a saint ..." His reserve is fascinating, given that it is preceded by the customary denunciation of the *Fuṣūṣ*. We are able to understand this ambiguous position via his comment that, "By God, it is better that a Muslim live behind his cows in ignorance [...] than possess this gnosis and subtle knowledge!"[3] Clearly, Dhahabī is not condemning the doctrine of Ibn ʿArabī as much as its diffusion among the 'mass of believers' (*ʿāmma*).

Nothing would be more contradictory to the reality of the situation than believing—or allowing someone to believe, as is the case with the Wahhābīs[4]—that all the *ʿulamā'* have condemned Ibn ʿArabī. Some Sufis have opposed the school of Ibn ʿArabī; on the other hand, a number of *ʿulamā'*, among whom are some of the most reputable, have come to his defence. Among these, Fīrūzābādī (d. 1414) who, in the Yemen, composed a *fatwā* in which he attempted to prove Ibn ʿArabī's holiness, and to commend Sultan al-Nāṣir for collecting Ibn ʿArabī's works. Less than a century later, in 1517, Kamāl Pashā Zādeh (d. 1534), close advisor to Salīm I, recommended that the Sultan, who had just conquered Egypt and who, as we have seen, played a role in Ibn ʿArabī's posthumous fate, reprimand those who disparage the Shaykh al-Akbar.

In mentioning Ibn ʿArabī's adversaries, we have deliberately omitted discussion of the propaganda against Ibn ʿArabī that is regularly published even today by the Wahhābīs and their emulators. The intellectual mediocrity of this pamphlet literature renders any comment on it unnecessary. But, ill-willed as it may be, the tenacity with

[3] *Mīzān al-iʿtidāl*, Beirut, 1963, vol. III, p. 660.

[4] The Wahhābī movement was founded in the eighteenth century by Muḥammad Ibn ʿAbd al-Wahhāb; it is a fundamentalist movement whose goal is to 'purify' Islam by eliminating, in particular, Sufism and the worship of saints.

which his work is attacked raises a question: is Ibn ʿArabī a 'vivifier of religion', as his traditional appellation (*Muḥyī al-dīn*) indicates, or is he, as his adversaries prefer to call him, a 'killer of religion' (*Mumīt al-dīn*)?

The Prince's Prayer

"SINCE I WAS old enough to wear a sword-belt, I did not cease mounting steeds, ... examining sabre blades, parading in military camps (*al-ᶜasākir*), instead of pouring over the pages of books."[1] It is doubtful that any of those who knew him well would have been able to predict that this boy who was so attracted to the clanking of military armour would soon devote himself to the strict renunciation of the ascetic. Everything pointed the young Ibn ᶜArabī toward a military career. The Spirit that blows where it wills had decided otherwise.

Ibn ᶜArabī's family was descended from one of the oldest Arab lineages in Muslim Spain. His ancestors, Arabs from the Yemen, emigrated toward the Iberian peninsula at quite an early date; most likely, during the 'second wave' of the conquest, the wave that, in 712, brought several thousand Yemenite horsemen into Andalusia. In any case, they were listed among the "great Arab families" that were living in Andalusia in the census that took place during the reign of the first Umayyad amīr (756-788). Thus, they belonged to the *khāṣṣa*, the ruling class that occupied the-

[1] *Dīwān al-maᶜārif*, ms. B.N. 2346, folio 36b.

highest offices in the administration and the army.[2]

Proud of his Arab origins, Ibn ʿArabī would recall, mostly in his poems, the name of his ancestor the famous Ḥātim al-Ṭā'ī, the pre-Islamic Arabian poet whose chivalrous virtues are proverbial. On the other hand, he alludes on a number of occasions to the important position of his father, who, he states, "was one of the Sultan's companions"[3]—a phrase that has given rise to much conjecture, and one which some recent biographers have used to conclude that he was at the very least a minister. A document published a few years ago now allows us a much clearer view. According to its author, Ibn Shaʿār (d. 1256), who met the Shaykh al-Akbar in Aleppo on 27 October 1237 and asked him about his youth, Ibn ʿArabī "was from a military family *in the service of those who govern the country*".[4] Although it is elusive, the phrase reminds us that the career of Ibn ʿArabī's father evolved within the framework of the political vicissitudes that accompanied the collapse of the Almoravid regime in Andalusia.

The Almoravids, who were Berber immigrants from the western Sahara, had arrived in the peninsula at the request of the Taifa sovereigns. The autonomous Taifa states had come into being after the fall of the caliphate in Cordoba, and they were then concerned about the continual advance of the Christians, who had taken Toledo in May 1085. The crushing defeat that the Almoravids inflicted on the

[2] See *Fut.*, I, pp. 506, 588-9; C. Addas, *Quest for the Red Sulphur. The Life of Ibn ʿArabī*, Cambridge, The Islamic Texts Society, 1993, pp. 48-49; originally published as *Ibn ʿArabī ou la Quête du Soufre Rouge*, Paris, Gallimard, 1989.

[3] *Rūḥ al-quds*, Damascus, 1970, p. 108.

[4] *ʿUqūd al-jumān*, in *al-Dirāsāt al-islāmiyya*, vol. 26, 1991, no. 1-2, p. 246. The italics here and throughout the book are the author's.

Castillians less than a year later in Zallāqa allowed the Almoravids to present themselves as the defenders of Andalusian Islam. Slowly but surely, they annexed the Taifas and finally established the first Andalu-Maghreban state, thus marking a new era in the history of Muslim Spain. From then on, their political, religious, and cultural destiny was closely linked to that of the Maghreb. A mosaic of ethnic groups, languages, and beliefs was gradually replaced by a more homogeneous, and mainly Arabicised and Islamicised society; but also with a society that had folded in upon itself.

The uneasiness caused by the Reconquista's successes favoured intolerance toward both Jews and Christians, who emigrated to the north in swarms. But this intolerance was also due in part to the dogmatic rigidity of the Mālikite jurists, whose ascendancy over the Almoravid sovereigns was considerable. Almoravid puritanism, the importance that they gave to jurisprudence at the expense of study of the Qur'ān and the *sunna*, the 'traditions of the Prophet', all gave birth to a pedantic casuistry that smothered any new religious aspirations—as can be seen most notably in the development of Sufism. It is thus significant that the two uprisings most responsible for undermining the regime's stability came in the form of religious reform movements.

After a stay in the East, where he was introduced to the works of Ghazālī, Ibn Tumart, a Berber from Sous, returned to the Maghreb to preach a more sombre Islam; an Islam centred on *tawḥīd*, the affirmation of divine Oneness—whence the name *muwaḥḥidūn* (and thus Almohads) that was given to his partisans. Fulminating against the Almoravid leaders, whom he accused of being anthropomorphists and infidels, he proclaimed himself to be the *Mahdī*—he who would help Jesus restore peace and justice at the end of the time—and took to arms. Upon his death, in 1130, ʿAbd al-Mu'min, one of his oldest followers, took over as his successor and continued the struggle. The war was long, and there were defeats, but the taking of Marrakech in 1147 put an end to Almoravid sovereignty in the Maghreb.

The annexation of Muslim Spain, where the Almoravids had fallen prey to serious interior difficulties, was more quick. An *autodafé* of Ghazālī's works was decreed by the authorities in Andalusia and stirred up a considerable amount of unrest among the people, particularly in Sufi circles. This unhappiness, which was accentuated by military defeats (the Almoravids lost Zaragoza in 1118), helped the expansion of the *murīdūn*. The *murīdūn* were a kind of congregation that gathered in Algarve around Ibn Qaṣī, who was claiming to be the Imām, the spiritual and political Guide of the community. Infatuated with the propaganda of the Almohads, from whom he was hoping for assistance, Ibn Qaṣī persuaded ʿAbd al-Mu'min to send troops into the Peninsula. The first of these arrived in 1146 and, one year later, Seville and the surrounding region were under Almohad rule. But the conquest was far from complete. Granada remained under Almoravid control; Almeria was occupied by the Castillians, while an independent emirate arose in the East under the protection of Ibn Mardanīsh, a military leader whose headquarters were in Murcia.

It was in Murcia, where his father exercised military duties in the service of Ibn Mardanīsh, that Ibn ʿArabī was born on 27 July 1165 (17 Ramaḍān 560), or, according to other sources, 6 August (27 Ramaḍān). Less than three months later, Murcia was besieged by the Almohads, although they were not able to take the city until March 1172. Ibn Mardanīsh did not survive the defeat; his sons, accompanied by a delegation of the army's highest officers, went to Seville where they pledged allegiance to the caliph Abū Yaᶜqūb Yūsuf. This Almohad sovereign, who had succeeded his father in 1163, quickly took Ibn Mardanīsh's generals into his service, for he was well aware of their competence. Ibn ᶜArabī's father had probably been among these officials, for it was at about this time that he emigrated to Seville to continue his career in the service of the Almohads. From that time on, nothing disturbed Ibn ᶜArabī's pleasantly carefree childhood. As a young boy he loved to hunt and, as we have seen, to play soldier. His future seemed assured; in imitation of his father, for he was an only son, he entered the army.

A Dazzling Metamorphosis

There is nothing that could have predicted that the life of this adolescent destined for a military career would go through such a radical change from one day to the next. We may never know exactly what happened, or precisely when. The famous text where he describes his interview in Cordoba with the philosopher Averroes provides at least one piece of chronological information. Ibn ᶜArabī describes himself as a still beardless young man, but one who had been granted illuminative knowledge during the course of a recent retreat (see box p. 16).

From this account it can be deducted that the event took place when he was about fifteen. What follows in Ibn Shaᶜār's account adds one more detailed piece of information regarding the circumstances of this short and precocious *metanoia*. "What led me to leave the army, on the one hand, and to take up the Path on the other hand," Ibn ᶜArabī told him, "was this: I had gone out one day with Prince Abū Bakr [b.] Yūsuf b. ᶜAbd al-Mu'min in Cordoba.

The Child and the Philosopher

I was in Cordoba one day at the home of *al-qāḍī* Abū al-Walīd Ibn Rushd [Averroes]. He had been astonished when he had heard about the illumination that God had bestowed upon me, and expressed a desire to meet me. Since my father was one of his friends, he found some excuse to send me to his house. At the time, I was a young boy with no hair on my face, not even a moustache. When I was led to him, he [Averroes] stood up, showed his affection and consideration, and kissed me. Then he said to me, "Yes." I, in turn, said, "Yes." His joy increased upon seeing that I understood what he was referring to. Thus, upon realising the reason for his joy, I added, "No." He cringed, lost his colour, and was overcome with doubt, "So, what have you found through the lifting of the veil and divine inspiration? Is it identical to what speculative thought gives us?" I replied, "Yes and no; between yes and no, spirits take to flight and necks are detached [from their bodies]."

Ibn ʿArabī, *Futūḥāt*, I, pp. 153-154

We went to the great mosque and I watched him while he bowed and prostrated himself in humble and contrite prayer. I then remarked to myself, 'If someone like this, who is no less than the sovereign of this country, is submissive and humble, and behaves in such a way towards God, it is because this lower world is nothing!' I left him that same day, never to see him again, and undertook the Path."

This document, however, raises as many questions as it answers. Ibn Shaʿār places this event in 1184, at which date Ibn ʿArabī would have been nineteen. But the picture that Ibn ʿArabī paints of himself in the account of his encounter with Averroes shows clearly that his first spiritual experiences had taken place long before this. Moreover, who is the prince in question? Caliph Yūsuf ruled between 1163 and 1184, and he could not have been in Cordoba at that time, since he left Andalusia in 1176 for Morocco, where he lived until 1184. He re-crossed the Strait of Gibraltar in May 1184, and proceeded directly to Seville to inspect the troops. Shortly thereafter, on 7 June, the caliph left the capital for an expedition against Portugal from which he did not return alive. Now, his 'patronym' was Abū Yaʿqūb (and not Abū Bakr), and Ibn ʿArabī would have been aware of this.[5] Given the information that we have, it is likely that the prince whose humility in prayer so moved Ibn ʿArabī was Abū Bakr, one of the caliph's sons and also one of his generals.

Whatever the case may be, one thing is for certain: the incident in the mosque in Cordoba constitutes a breaking point in the previously peaceful existence of the young Ibn ʿArabī. The grain of sand that came to upset the course of his life unleashed an attack of conscience that was as brutal as it was irreversible. His decision was made: he chose God. The adolescent left everything, the army, his companions, his wealth. He withdrew from the world—into a cave located in the middle of a cemetery, according to one of his biographers—for a face-to-face encounter with the Eternal from which, in a way, he never returned. "I began my retreat before dawn and I received illumination before sunrise [...] I remained in this place for fourteen months, and I obtained secrets about which I later wrote; my spiritual opening, at that moment, was an ecstatic uprooting."[6]

5 In *al-Durra al-fākhira* Ibn ʿArabī mentions the Almohad sovereign whom he calls "caliph Abū Yaʿqūb". See R.W.J. Austin (trans.), *Sufis of Andalusia. The Rūḥ al-quds and al-durrat al-fākirah of Ibn ʿArabī*, London, 1971, no. 56.

6 *Kitāb wasā'il al-sā'il*, M. Profitlich (ed.), Freiburg, 1973, p. 21.

A tremendous metamorphosis, in the strongest sense of this word, thus took place in this young man. When he came out of his seclusion, he had nothing in common with the adolescent who used to wander through military garrisons but his name. Aware of this radical split between what he had been up till then and what he was later to become, Ibn ʿArabī referred to his prior way of living as "my *jāhiliyya*", the same word that is used to refer to the state of paganism—literally, 'ignorance'—in which the Arabs lived before the revelation to Muḥammad that ushered in the new era of their destiny.

"Flee towards God"

THE DAZZLING ILLUMINATION that Ibn ʿArabī experienced during the first hours of his retreat conforms to what in Muslim mystical language is referred to as a 'rapture' (*jadhba*). The *majdhūb*, the 'enraptured', is, in a sense, torn by God out of his ordinary condition without passing through the steps of a long and painful discipline. In order for this form of flashing and passive spiritual realisation to be complete, it must be followed by the *via purgativa*,[1] "the highest and the most perfect path", according to Amīr ʿAbd al-Qādīr, a nineteenth-century representative of Ibn ʿArabī's school. 'Desired' by God (*murād*), he who is blessed with the *jadhba* must become a 'desirer' (*murīd*), and step by step tread the path of perfection over which he had already flown.

Ibn ʿArabī points out in a number of passages that in his experience a vision played a decisive role.[2] The longest and most complete account of this event is found in a passage from *The Collection of Divine Knowledge* where he recalls

[1] According to a traditional schema in mystical theology, this expression refers to the first of the three degrees of the path towards perfection, that which leads to purification of the soul. The two degrees that follow it are the 'illuminative way', and the 'unitive way'.

[2] *Fut.*, II, p. 491; IV, p. 172.

his childhood memories, "I lived like this until the Merciful turned His care towards me, sending Muḥammad, Jesus, and Moses to me in my sleep, may the grace and peace of God be upon them! Jesus urged me to take up a life of asceticism and renunciation. Moses gave me the 'disk of the sun' and told me that from among the science of 'Unicity' (*tawḥīd*) I would obtain 'knowledge from God' (*al-ᶜilm al-ladunī*). And Muḥammad commanded, 'Hold fast to me and you shall be safe!' I awoke in tears and devoted the rest of the night to chanting the Qur'ān. I then resolved to dedicate myself to God's Path ..."[3] This subtly experienced encounter with the representatives of the main monotheistic traditions presages the universal quality of Ibn ᶜArabī's teaching, and marks the starting point of what truly appears to be his spiritual commitment (*tawba*), and his conversion in the strict sense of the word.[4]

It must be acknowledged that the documents that are presently available to us make precise dating of this event impossible. As a matter of fact, the 'conversion' of a saint—regardless of the religion that he or she belongs to—can rarely be dated precisely. This long and complex interior process entails a series of more or less distinct stages that can be, and often are, interrupted by periods of abatement (*fatra*), of turning back, or of hesitation.[5] What is certain is that Ibn ᶜArabī's conversion, properly speaking, took place later than the illumination (*fatḥ*) he experienced just before his meeting with Averroes.

[3] *Dīwān al-maᶜārif*, folio 36b.

[4] See Addas, *Quest for the Red Sulphur*, pp. 41-42.

[5] Ibn ᶜArabī recounts his experience of this in *Fut.*, IV, p. 172; cf. Addas, *Quest for the Red Sulphur*, p. 43.

In the Footsteps of the Prophet

Muḥammad's injunction could not have been clearer: imitation of the Prophet is the one and only way to reach spiritual perfection. Following Muḥammad's example is a fundamental precept in Islamic hagiology—one whose scriptural source may be found in verse 21 of Sūra 33, "In the Messenger of God you have an excellent example." In fact, for Muslim mystics conformity to the Muḥammadan example is the *sine qua non* of all spiritual realisation being both its means and its end. In their eyes, the Messenger of God who appears at a precise moment in history as the 'Seal of the Prophets', is also, on the cosmic scale, the Perfect Man (*al-insān al-kāmil*). In other words, he is the paradigm of sainthood; he is the being in whom sainthood achieves its plenitude. Imitation of the Prophet cannot be reduced to copying his deeds and his movements; it implies in-depth knowledge of his 'customs' (*sunna*). The young Ibn ʿArabī, whose book knowledge was limited to the Qur'ān, was well aware of this. Thus, he began his study of *ḥadīth* (that fundamental branch of religious teaching that concerns Muḥammad's acts and words) with the most reputable teachers. Ibn ʿArabī would continue his study of *ḥadīth* until the day he died. It should be emphasised that the importance he placed on this study, and even more so on *practising* the *sunna*, was in Ibn ʿArabī's case not a pious concession in conformity with the Islamic society in which he lived: it was part and parcel of his hagiological, as well as his initiatory teaching.

If the theme of the spiritual pre-eminence of Muḥammad was present long before Ibn ʿArabī's time, it was nevertheless to him that we are indebted for a precise and rigorous summary of the nature and function of Muḥammadan excellence. Chapter three hundred and thirty-seven of the *Futūḥāt*, which is dedicated to 'Muḥammad's abode', contains essential details that pertain to this matter. "The Prophet received specific privileges that have never been given to any other prophet before; but no prophet has received a privilege that was not given in equal measure to Muḥammad, since he received the 'Sum of Words'. He said, 'I was a prophet when Adam was between clay and water', while the other prophets became prophets only at the time of their historical manifestation. [...] It is because of this that he is the one who assists every Perfect Man, whether he is the beneficiary of a revealed Law or the beneficiary of inspired knowledge [...] When he appeared, he was like the sun in which all light is lost [...]. His rank in wisdom encompasses the knowledge of all those who know God among the first and among the last [...]. His Law includes all men without exception, and his mercy, by virtue of which he was sent, embraces the whole universe [...]. His community (*umma*) encompasses all beings, as he was sent to them all; whether they believe in him or not, *all beings are included*..."[6]

Three key ideas, which are already to be found in writings from Ibn ʿArabī's youth, in for example, the *Divine Ordonnances* (*al-Tadbīrāt al-ilāhiyya*), appear in the above extract from the *Futūḥāt*. There is firstly the idea of the pre-existence of Muḥammad, more precisely the 'Muḥammadan Reality'. Since Muḥammad was the first being to be brought into existence from the *materia prima*, the Muḥammadan Reality begins the cosmological process and is its end. Secondly, the prophets that have been sent one after another to humanity are only sporadic and fragmentary manifestations of the Muḥammadan Reality,

[6] *Fut.*, III, pp. 141-144.

which is fully displayed only in the person of Muḥammad whose revelation encompasses and perfects the realities of all those that preceded it. This is why he refers to the universality of Muḥammad's message, which is addressed to all human beings without exception, whether they hold to it or not. And finally, the primordial and universal nature of the Muḥammadan Reality includes its supreme perfection; it is the untarnished mirror of divine perfections, the unique source from which all sainthood springs and into which it is reabsorbed. The idea of a Muḥammadan Reality conveyed by one prophet after another up to the point of its total blossoming in the historical person of Muḥammad appeared very early in Sufism. It was, however, articulated in ways that were more allusive than explicit. It is in the writings of Ibn ʿArabī that we find for the first time a detailed explanation of the idea. Ibn ʿArabī draws practical consequences out of what were previously abstract considerations. Since Muḥammad is the archetype of sainthood, it is in strict conformity to his *sunna*, and by taking nourishment from his example, that the aspirant manages to restore his original nature of *imago Dei*.

"God created Adam in His own image", says a famous *ḥadīth*. Likewise, man virtually has all the Divine Names engraved in the very clay of his being. It is because of this divine similitude that God has called him to be His *khalīfa*, his 'vicegerent' on earth. "Vicegerency (*khilāfa*) was assigned to Adam, to the exclusion of the other creatures of the universe, because God created him according to His image. A vicegerent must possess the attributes of the one he represents; otherwise he is not truly a vicegerent."[7] But these two favours granted exclusively to man, his divine

[7] *Fut.*, I, p. 263.

form and his governance, simultaneously expose him to the greatest danger of his existence: the illusion of sovereignty. As the Shaykh al-Akbar points out on a number of occasions, being conscious of his original theomorphism leads man to forget that he was created from clay—the most humble of substances and a symbol of his 'ontological servitude' (*ʿubūdiyya*). The power and the authority that his mandate grant him lead him to consider himself autonomous. He appropriates sovereignty, which rightfully belongs only to Him Whom he represents, and he betrays the oath of vassalage that he made when he replied to the question "Am I Not your Lord?" with "Certainly, we are witnesses!"[8]

When he refuses to assume his status as 'servant of God' (*ʿabd Allāh*), he is henceforth unworthy of being 'God's vicegerent' (*khalīfat Allāh*). "The homeland of man is his servitude; he who leaves it is forbidden to take on the Divine Names."[9] To regain his original nobility, he must reactivate the divine characteristics inscribed in his primordial form; characteristics that his pretension and ignorance had covered up. "The Prophet said, 'I have come to complete the 'noble character traits.'" He who lives in accordance with the 'noble character traits' follows a law of God even if he is not aware of it [...] To perfect one's character means to strip it of all that tends to give it a vile status. Actually, vile characteristics are vile only by accident, while noble characteristics are noble by essence, for what is vile has no foundation in the divine [...], while noble characteristics do have foundation in the divine. The Prophet perfected the noble character traits to the extent that he established the ways through which a character can maintain a noble

[8] Qur'ān 7:172.
[9] *Fut.*, I, pp. 362, 367.

status and be exempt from a vile status."[10]

Underlying this passage is a major theme in Ibn ʿArabī's teaching: it is by the strictest and most absolute observance of Divine Law that man is able to re-establish his original theomorphism. Every quality, including for example jealousy and anger, is noble in essence, since each has its root in a divine attribute. A quality becomes 'ignoble' and reprehensible only to the extent that it exists outside the limits imposed by the Law. Consequently, it is in conforming to the Prophet's *sunna* and to the Law that was revealed to him that man re-integrates in himself the divine characteristics that lie dormant deep within him.

The Disciple of Jesus

The deep veneration that Ibn ʿArabī had for Jesus—to whom, as we shall see, he attributes a major role in his hierarchy of sainthood—will undoubtedly seem paradoxical for a master who, on the other hand, continually claims the quality of "perfect follower of Muḥammad" and even goes so far as to call himself "Muḥammad's supreme heir". A brief analysis of his hagiological doctrine and of the important underlying concept of prophetic heritage quickly shows that there is no contradiction. Also, the Shaykh al-Akbar's devotion to the person of Jesus was not born out of abstract speculation; its source lies in the intimate relationship established from the very beginning between the young adolescent searching for God and the Son of Mary. "He [Jesus] is my first master on the Way; *it is in his hands that I was converted*. He watches over me at all hours, not leaving me for even a second."[11] Another passage from the *Futūḥāt* gives a fuller understanding of why Ibn ʿArabī at times asso-

[10] *Fut.*, II, p. 562.
[11] *Fut.*, III, p. 341.

ciates his conversion with the vision that placed him in the presence of the three prophets, and at other times attributes it solely to Jesus' intervention, "I often met him in my visions; it was with him that I repented. [...] He commanded me to practice asceticism and renunciation."[12] If Muḥammad had laid out the itinerary that he was to follow, it was Jesus who, during the same visionary episode, presented himself as his guide on the long and perilous journey that he was to undertake. It was he who, in the absence of an earthly master, took care of the education of the young mystic who was not yet exposed to the detours and the perils of the Way.

Without his then being completely conscious of the fact, Ibn ʿArabī's fate was henceforth linked in more than one way to that of his invisible protector, Jesus, whose recommendations he carried out to the letter. "Thus I stripped myself of everything I possessed. And yet, *at that time I had no master* to whom I might turn over my affairs and give my goods. So, I went to my father; after consulting him, I gave him all that I owned. I called upon no one else, for I did not come back to God through the intercession of a master, since at that time I did not know any. *I separated myself from my goods like a dead man separates from his family and his possessions.*"[13]

Although this is not the most common form of spiritual direction, the [indirect] spiritual influence of a prophet, or of a dead spiritual master, is not unheard of. In Sufi vocabulary, it confers on those who hold it the status of *uwaysī*—referring to the case of Uways al-Qaranī, a contemporary of the Prophet who was instructed by Muḥammad even though the two never met. The *uwaysī*

[12] *Fut.*, II, p. 49.
[13] *Fut.*, II, p. 548.

thus constitute a category of saints who possess a kind of 'spontaneous generation', since their [spiritual] genealogies are irregular. This explains those isolated cases that occasionally show up in initiatory chains where someone appears as the disciple of a master who died a century before the disciple's birth. Even if he subsequently met a number of *shuyūkh* (pl. of *skaykh*) and profited from their teachings, Ibn ʿArabī remained an *uwaysī* up to his dying breath.

As we shall see, Ibn ʿArabī started to keep company with spiritual masters in 1184, when he was nineteen years of age. His decision to give up wordly possessions was thus made previously, at a time when, under the tutelage of the Son of Mary, he walked the path toward God in the greatest of solitude. Curiously, his father, whose religious zeal at the time was in no way comparable to that of his son, does not appear to have been opposed to this radical withdrawal from the world. Such a course of action could not easily have gone unnoticed by his acquaintances. Granted, there were family records of two similarly spectacular conversions at an earlier time. Before Ibn ʿArabī was born, there was the case of one of his maternal uncles, a Berber prince who, in the Almoravid era, reigned for a time over Tlemcen. The story of this amīr who, moved by the recriminations of an ascetic he had unwisely rebuked, immediately exchanged his royal robes for the Sufi frock, had certainly stirred popular imagination. Consequently, one is hardly surprised to find the account of this dramatic conversion, which Ibn ʿArabī recorded in the *Futūḥāt*,[14] in Tādilī's (d. 1230) hagiographical collection or in the history of the Tlemcen kings composed by the brother of the famous his-

[14] *Fut.*, II, p. 18.

torian Ibn Khaldūn.

Even more moving is the story that Ibn ʿArabī tells, relying on his own childhood memories, about his father's brother.[15] This uncle was passing peacefully into old age when, at the apothecary, he encountered a young boy looking for some medicine. The alarming ignorance in matters of pharmacology displayed by the child became the subject of an unfortunate joke on the part of the old man. The boy—who, Ibn ʿArabī points out, showed signs of being a pious worshipper—replied that his unfamiliarity with drugs was minuscule compared to the old man's lack of concern in matters relating to God, "My uncle," Ibn ʿArabī recounts, "took this admonition to heart; he put himself in the child's service and, through him, entered the Way."

As it happened, Ibn ʿArabī's father, did disapprove of his son's too marked religious tendencies. However, he did come round to his son's point of view toward the end of his life, "The day that he died, and he was gravely ill at the time, he sat up completely without support and said, 'My child, today is a day of departure and encounter.' I replied, 'God has ordained your salvation in this journey, and He blesses you in this encounter.' He rejoiced in my words and said, 'May God reward you! My child, *everything I heard you say and that I did not understand, and which I sometimes rejected, is now my profession of faith*.'"[16]

Even though he had resolved to renounce worldly possessions at a time when he was still an adolescent, Ibn ʿArabī's rejection of his father's possessions had not been the result of a fickle juvenile enthusiasm. Made after deep consideration, his decision was the result of simple observa-

[15] Austin, *Sufis of Andalusia*, no. 13, pp. 99-100.
[16] *Fut.*, I, p. 222.

tion: indigence (*faqr*) is the inescapable status of created beings; a status defined by the Qur'ānic verse that he so often quoted, "O men! You are indigent in the face of God!"[17] It is because of his denial of this ontological indigence that man fell from his original theomorphism; it is in accepting indigence that his theomorphism can be recovered. Another autobiographical account confirms that Ibn ᶜArabī's 'renunciation' was, to his mind, nothing more than the strict application of metaphysical law that governs all beings, "Since the moment I attained this spiritual station [that of 'pure servitude'], I have not owned any living creature; nor do I own even the clothes that I wear, for I wear only what is lent to me and what I am allowed to use. If something fell into my possession, I would immediately get rid of it by giving it away, or, in the case of a slave, by freeing him. I took this upon myself when I chose to aspire to supreme servitude in God's eyes. And then it was said to me, 'That will not be possible for you so long as one single being has the right to claim something from you!' I replied, 'God Himself could claim nothing from me!' In response to this I was asked, 'How can this be?' And I answered, 'One claims only from those who deny [their ontological indigence], not from those who recognise [it]; one claims from those who maintain that they have rights and goods, not of those who declare, "I have no right, anywhere, to anything!"'"[18]

The comparison that Ibn ᶜArabī makes between abandoning his goods and death is thus not just a simple metaphor. It is evidence of the profound significance of his spiritual commitment, such as he conceived it to be. The flight toward God ordained by verse 50 of Sūra 51, "Flee

[17] Qur'ān 35:15.
[18] *Fut.*, I. p. 196.

towards God!" leads the pilgrim toward the death of the ego. The voyage that he undertakes is, like that of the dead person, a voyage of no return and he must make it in complete nakedness.

The Masters of the Way

THE INCREASINGLY AUDACIOUS raids perpetrated by the Christian garrisons in Andalusia and the pillaging to which the rural population was subjected gradually created a pervasive climate of insecurity in the Peninsula. A look at the hagiographical sources of the period is most informative. The recurrent mention of the *Rūm* (the Christians), the accounts of their attacks, on land as well as by sea, and of the miraculous deliverance of saints held captive by them, all give testimony to the precariousness of the Andalusian situation. The Santarem debacle in July 1184, in which Caliph Yūsuf was mortally wounded, brought popular uneasiness to its climax.

When he succeeded his father, Caliph Yaʿqūb attempted to remedy the situation by re-establish moral order. As soon as he took the throne, he ordered the seizure of all supplies of alcohol, he decreed that anyone who drank alcohol would be put to death, he mandated the expulsion of the singers on the banks of the Guadalquivir, and he, himself, acted as judge at public hearings. He was, however, soon forced to deal with revolts that were breaking out in North Africa, where the Almoravids from the Balearic Islands were attempting to regain power. After retaking Algiers and Bougie, Yaʿqūb won an important victory in 1187.

This success was, nonetheless, not sufficient to put an end to the Almoravid counter-offensive; they continued to stir up trouble for decades to follow. In the Iberian Peninsula, his military undertakings against the Christians would be more successful, ultimately earning for him the title *Manṣūr*, 'the Victorious'. His successes were, however, not as decisive as his contemporaries tended to believe; the victory in Alarcos in 1195 only temporarily held back the inexorable progress of the Reconquista.

The Heroism of the Andalusian Sufis

"I became the companion of men faithful to the pact they had sealed with God, I kept the company of spiritual teachers who, from the moment they turned in His direction, never again turned away. I have greatly benefited from my service to them, and because of their spiritual energy I received the 'subtle secrets'." [1] At the death of Caliph Yūsuf in 1184, Ibn ʿArabī was only nineteen. It was at this time, he says in the *Futūḥāt*, that he entered the Way. The word *ṭarīq* that he uses in this passage—which strictly speaking means 'road'—is not to be confused with the word *rujūʿ* or *tawba*, 'return', which he uses to refer to his conversion itself and which is linked, as we have seen, to his encounter with the three prophets Jesus, Moses and Muḥammad. What is here intended is the 'Way of the masters'. In other words, it was during the year 1184 that Ibn ʿArabī began to keep the company of *shuyūkh*, and to follow their teachings.

The solitary adoration of the One God was thus followed by contemplation of His theophanies in creatures. Ibn ʿArabī's return toward the society of men ushered in a new stage in his spiritual destiny, one which would be long and

[1] *Dīwān al-maʿārif*, folio 36b.

rich. During the ensuing years, he was to encounter a considerable number of saints (*awliyā'*), and he was to frequent the most famous representatives of Andalusian and Maghreban Sufism. There is no question that his work was marked by this mystical environment and that his teachings drew deeply from the tradition he inherited from his spiritual masters. And yet, it is also true that when Ibn ʿArabī met the men and women whose attentive and devoted companion he was to be, he was far from being a novice. In the solitude of his retreats, in the silence of his prayers, he had advanced greatly along the path. And the young man who one day showed up at the dwelling of Shaykh ʿUryanī, who was to become his first 'earthly' guide, was already radiating the astounding knowledge which, enriched by the numerous encounters and experiences that marked the stages of his journey from Seville to Mecca, would later fill the pages of the *Futūḥāt al-makkiyya*.

Conscious of the exceptional qualities of his masters, Ibn ʿArabī, even before leaving his native land, transcribed the unforgettable moments spent in their company. Unfortunately, this volume has never been found. But upon his arrival in Egypt, where he, for the first time, discovered the landscape of Eastern Sufism—a landscape which was quite different from that of the West—Ibn ʿArabī took true measure of how the universe of the Andalusian and Maghreban spiritual masters he had left behind was both marvellous and unique. He had barely set foot in Cairo when a shaykh, a native of Iraq, asserted in his presence that there were no authentic gnostics in the West. An immediate verbal reply, courteous though firm, was followed two years later by his *Epistle on the Spirit of Sainthood* (*Rūḥ al-quds*), a vibrant testimonial to the high degree of sanctity of his Western masters. Then, as if that has not been enough to immortalise the memory of these heroes (*fityān*)—for they were, in his eyes, heroes—he later dedicated a third work to them, and gave it the same title as the first book of which it was an abridgement, *The Precious Pearl (al-Durra al-fākhira)*.[2]

Given that there are few first hand accounts of Andalusian Sufism, the *Rūḥ* and the *Durra* provide us with primary sources for the history of Sufi thought of this period. The seventy-one entries that make up the two volumes extant today paint a lively and colourful panorama of the Andalusian Sufi world at the end of the twelfth century. However, Ibn ʿArabī was not attempting to compose a hagiographical work; nor was it his intention to edify his reader by an enumeration of wonders, but rather to depict sainthood in its most pared down and in its most unexpected forms. If some of his saints did manage to appear in prestigious biographical dictionaries like Ibn al-ʿAbbār's (d. 1259), it was sometimes because of their ascetic qualities, but more often due to their competence in the areas of exoteric religious sciences (their knowledge of *ḥadīth*, for example), or because of their fame in the literary domain, and in poetry in particular. The mission of these compilers was to record the lives of notable personages and to celebrate local greatness. But the majority of the spiritual masters described by Ibn ʿArabī were unknown individuals who could not be differentiated from ordinary people. They were artisans and shopkeepers; they were poor. Who would suspect that these common people had privileged contact with God? *Sufis of Andalusia* offers a dazzling portrait of the simplest and most brilliant sainthood hidden

[2] The *Rūḥ* and the *Durra* were partially translated in *Sufis of Andalusia*.

behind dark, and often destitute, silhouettes.

ʿUryanī, the first of the masters to whom Ibn ʿArabī turned, was an illiterate peasant who could neither write nor count. And yet, he was capable of the subtlest commentaries on the maxims that make up *The Beauties of Spiritual Sessions*, a work by Ibn al-ʿArīf, the famous Andalusian Sufi (d. 1141). Nevertheless, his name, in Ibn ʿArabī's opinion, is more closely connected with the idea of 'servitude' (*ʿubūdiyya*) that was so central to his teaching. Other spiritual masters were certainly more knowledgeable than ʿUryanī, but none of them were great theoreticians of Sufism. Their teachings may have contained references to doctrine, but, above all, they emphasised practice. Mīrtulī was an educated man—even if he only held the position of *imām* in a small mosque—and his collection of mystical poems earned him a place in the *Takmila*. Ibn ʿArabī, however, admired his poetic talent less than his overwhelming compassion for his neighbours, "When someone was in need, he [Mīrtulī] sold a book from his quite substantial library so that the unfortunate may have food from the proceeds of the sale [...] When his last book was sold, he died ..."[3] Ibn ʿArabī's memory of Abū Ḥasan al-Shakkāz was that he never said 'me'; "Never once did I hear him utter the word."[4] Fāṭima, who was eighty-four when he met her, ate the food scraps that the people of Seville left in front of their doors; when she found neither alms nor scraps, she exclaimed, "Oh Lord! To what do I owe this high rank, that You should treat me the same way that You treat Your loved ones?"[5] His comment about Shaykh al-Qabā'ilī was that "his prayers could be heard by all creatures of the land

[3] Austin, *Sufis of Andalusia*, no. 8, p. 80.
[4] Ibid., no. 12, p. 88.
[5] Ibid., no. 55, p. 140.

and the sea, including the fish of the sea".[6]

Such examples can be multiplied, for Ibn ʿArabī was deeply marked by the humility, the simplicity, and the renunciation of Andalusia's spiritual adepts. Undoubtedly, these characteristics were to his mind the cardinal virtues of the hero (*fatā*), in the sense that Qushayrī gives to the word; "The hero is he who smashes idols and the idol of every man is his ego"—a definition inspired by the Qur'ānic story where Abraham, after destroying the idols worshipped by his people, is referred to by this word. In the chapter of the *Futūḥāt* dedicated to heroes (*fityān*, plural of *fatā*) and to 'heroic generosity' (*futuwwa*), the Shaykh al-Akbar abruptly affirms that, "The 'hero' is he who does not perform a single useless gesture."[7] Those who have reached this degree of spiritual development are "princes in the guise of slaves"; just as God provides sustenance for the impious, so do 'heroes' treat all creatures with kindness, regardless of how wrongly they may have been treated themselves. And citing the famous *ḥadīth*, "The master is at the service of those over whom he is master," Ibn ʿArabī comments that, "He whose authority consists in serving others is a 'pure servant' of God (*ʿabd maḥḍ*)."

The 'Way of Blame' and Absolute Servitude

Taken to its most extreme degree, 'heroic generosity' is but another name for *ʿubūdiyya*, 'servitude', to the extent that it is fully integrated and actualised by man. In fact, there is no question of acquiring 'servitude', as it is the indefeasible status of all creatures. The fundamental difference between the 'hero' and a normal believer is that the hero is forever

[6] Ibid., no. 20, p. 114.

[7] *Fut.*, I, p. 242.

conscious of his ontological indigence; there is nothing left in him that can hide it. "Nothing is more removed from the master than his slave; the condition of servitude, in itself, is not a state of proximity, but the consciousness that the slave has of his servitude brings him closer to his master."[8] In this regard, Ibn ʿArabī loves to cite the story in which the famous ninth century Sufi, Abū Yazīd al-Bisṭāmī, asked God how he could draw nearer to Him. The answer he received was, "Approach me through that which is not Mine: humility and indigence."

In his vow of servitude, in the eradication of any pretence of autonomy, man reaches *walāya*, a word usually translated by 'sainthood', but which literally means *proximity* to God. Having smashed the idol of the ego, he discovers that he only acts through God, as a *ḥadīth qudsī*[9] of which Ibn ʿArabī was so fond, states, "My servant draws near to Me by nothing I like more than by the works that I have prescribed for him. And he does not cease approaching Me by supererogatory works until I love him. And when I love him, I am his ear with which he hears, his sight with which he sees, his hand with which he grasps, his foot with which he walks ..." The real metamorphosis that comes about, says Ibn ʿArabī, is in he perception of the servant who, by virtue of engaging in supererogatory acts, becomes conscious that God is—and has never ceased being—his hearing, his sight ...

As sublime as this degree of spiritual realisation may be, it is nevertheless marked by imperfection, by the trace of individual will which helps the servant to perform acts of supererogation: acts *chosen by the servant himself*. In other

[8] *Fut.*, II, p. 561.

[9] The *ḥadīth qudsī* are words of God transmitted by Muḥammad, but which are not part of the Qur'ān.

words, he reserves for himself some measure of autonomy, as infinitesimal as this may be. For the 'pure servant', the possibility of a personal choice has disappeared. Consequently, he adheres to those works that God has imposed upon him and at the times that He imposes them on him. The 'abandonment of self-reliance' (to use the wonderful title of a mystical treatise by the fourteenth-century Egyptian saint, Ibn ʿAṭā Allāh) is his permanent state. Paradoxically, it is through this abdication of the powers that he attributes to himself that man qualifies to reign over the world as promised by God him when He set him up as 'vicegerent'. In effect, when he arrives at this station, as Ibn ʿArabī explains, it is no longer God who is "his ear, his sight ..."; it is he who, from that moment on, is the hearing and the sight of God. "God wills, through his will, *without him knowing that what he wants is exactly what God wants*; if he becomes conscious of it, he has not fully realised this station."[10] Completely extinguished to himself in the radiant Divine Presence, lost in the contemplation of the Divine Names, he no longer knows that he is. "When the servant has been stripped of all his names, those that confer his ontological servitude upon him as well as those that his original theomorphism grant him, nothing remains but his essence *devoid of either name or quality*. Then he is among 'those who are near' [...] Nothing is manifest either in him or by him that is not God."[11] Just like Abū Yazīd, this saint when he is asked, "How are you this morning?" will answer, "I have no qualities, I have neither morning nor evening."

Taking this into account, it is hardly surprising that Ibn

[10] *Fut.* IV, p. 559.
[11] *Fut.*, IV, p. 13.

ʿArabī assimilates 'heroes' with *malāmiyya*, the 'men of blame' who, according to him, "have donned the highest spiritual degree". The characteristics that he attributes to the *malāmiyya* in the chapter of the *Futūḥāt* dedicated to them are strikingly reminiscent of the portrait of his own spiritual masters, "They do not distinguish themselves from other believers through anything that would make them noticed [...]. They isolate themselves with God and never stray from their servitude; they are pure slaves, devoted to their Master. They are in permanent contemplation of Him, be they drinking, eating, awake or asleep [...] They seem to depend on things, for in everything, whatever be its name, they see but one Named: God. They hold fast, both inwardly and outwardly, to the name that God has given them: that of *indigent*. Since they know that God has hidden Himself from His creatures, they, too, hide from them."[12]

Contrary to the ascetics, whose efforts to renounce the world reveal that the world still has value in their eyes; and contrary to certain Sufis whose *charismata* are too visible, the *malāmiyya* intentionally fade into the deepest anonymity, that which constitutes every man's epitaph: 'servant of God'.

The Tribe of Saints

The countless references to, and anecdotes about, Andalusian Sufis found scattered throughout Ibn ʿArabī's writings, particularly in the *Futūḥāt*, are sufficient evidence of his deep devotion to his spiritual masters. In his eyes, these individuals were living evidence of *taṣawwuf*: Sufism in its noblest and most authentic aspect. But these refer-

[12] *Fut.*, III, p. 35.

ences also show that, in the case of Ibn ʿArabī, the master-disciple relationship was more complex than usual.

Let us take the example of Shaykh al-Kūmī, who in more than one way played an important role in Ibn ʿArabī's journey. In the first place, it was he who first brought to his attention mystical writings, the existence of which Ibn ʿArabī claimed he was yet unaware; "I did not even know the meaning of the word *taṣawwuf*."[13] Like many an *uwaysī*, Ibn ʿArabī was also *ummī*, an 'illiterate' saint. Of course, he knew how to read and write; he was equally well-versed in poetry, the Qur'ān, and *ḥadīth*, which he began to study after his conversion. But his spiritual knowledge, up to the time that he met Shaykh al-Kūmī, in 1190, was exclusively drawn from his own experience. In the absence of any book knowledge, or any intellectual references whatsoever, his perception of divine mysteries was completely virginal. This same master taught him the traditional rules of the Way, "He is the only one of my teachers who taught me any discipline."[14] But he immediately added, "He assisted me in initiatory discipline, and I assisted him with the ecstatic states; he was, for me, both a master and a student, and I was the same for him."

Despite the depth of his respect for his masters, Ibn ʿArabī was not afraid to contradict their point of view when the case arose. Convinced "by an infallible perception" that ʿUryanī was mistaken when he claimed to recognise the Mahdī in one of his contemporaries, Ibn ʿArabī openly disagreed, thus offending his teacher. On the way back to his house, a mysterious stranger approached him and reminded him of the sacrosanct rule of submission that a disciple

[13] *Rūḥ*, p. 80.
[14] *Fut.*, I, p. 616.

owes to his master. Ibn ᶜArabī immediately returned to ᶜUryanī to beg his forgiveness. But before he could get the first word out of his mouth, ᶜUryanī stopped him, "Am I going to have to ask Khaḍir to remind you of the rule of submission every time you contradict me?"[15]

An immortal traveller—for he had drunk at the Spring of Life—Khaḍir is the individual who, in the Sūra of the 'Cave', tests the wisdom and the patience of the prophet Moses and reveals to him the 'knowledge of My abode' (*ᶜilm ladunī*), the abode which God grants directly to some of His servants, and which Moses had predicted for Ibn ᶜArabī (see above). But the role of Khaḍir in the sphere of sainthood is not limited to impromptu interventions in the lives of the saints. According to Ibn ᶜArabī, he also has an important function at the very core of the invisible hierarchy without which the universe could not subsist.[16]

Potentially, 'vicegerency' belongs to all of Adam's progeny, but actually it belongs only to the saints, for it is they who, to all degrees and in all dimensions of the created universe, are the agents of the divine plan. Ibn ᶜArabī is not the only one to have had the idea of an 'Assembly of Saints' (*dīwān al-awliyā'*) with the permanent responsibility of making sure that cosmic equilibrium is maintained. But, as with a number of other ideas, it is he who has supplied the most complete and the most precise details that the Islamic tradition has to offer.

For Ibn ᶜArabī, all those who fulfil a *function* in this

[15] *Fut.*, I. p. 186.

[16] On this subject, cf. Michel Chodkiewicz, *Seal of the Saints. Prophethood and Sainthood in the Doctrine of Ibn ᶜArabī*, Cambridge, The Islamic Texts Society, 1993, chapter 4; originally published as *Le Sceau des saints. Prophétie and sainteté dans la doctrine d'Ibn Arabī*, Paris, Gallimard, 1986.

supreme pleroma, belong, by virtue of their spiritual degree, to the category of *malāmiyya*, and more specifically to that of the 'solitary ones' (*afrād*), who are its élite. The 'solitary ones' are, among men, homologous to the angels; like the cherubim, "stricken with love in contemplation of the Divine Majesty". None has authority over them except God, and it is He alone who gives them instruction. This explains Moses' confusion at Khaḍir's strange behaviour in Sūra 18. Some of the 'solitary ones' receive, by divine mandate, one of these functions that guarantee the cosmic order. Others are definitely hidden from the eyes of men. But all have made supreme servitude a reality; activated by the divine Will, they are like the stone that falls wherever it is thrown.[17]

The degree to which they have attained and the cosmic function they fulfil are two criteria by which saints are categorised. To this criteria is added that of the spiritual type that characterises a saint, and which determines his 'prophetic heritage'. Some saints are 'Christic'; others 'Abrahamic', 'Mosaic', and so forth. It frequently happens that a saint accumulates several prophetic heritages; such is the case, as we shall see, with Ibn ʿArabī. The prophetic 'ancestry' of a saint is a kind of genetic marker that determines in a characteristic manner the nature of his spiritual knowledge, his predominant virtues, his special *charismata*. Thus, a 'Christic' saint, and this type is one to which Ibn ʿArabī devotes no less than two entire chapters of the *Futūḥāt*, often has the ability to walk on water like Jesus did; he shows universal compassion for created beings, and the predominance of the attribute of divine mercy in him allows him to see what is best in all beings.

[17] *Fut.*, I, p. 710.

Primarily 'Christic'—which is not surprising, given the decisive role he attributes to Jesus at the beginning of his vocation—Ibn ʿArabī maintains that he was then received into the heritage of Moses, and then into that of all the other prophets, and finally into that of Muḥammad. Here it is important to remember that though a saint may be the heir of a particular prophet, in the last resort he is the heir of Muḥammad. Since the Muḥammadan Reality is the unique and perennial source of sainthood, it incorporates all the forms sainthood of which the successive prophets are eminent types. Moreover, in the *Futūḥāt*, Ibn ʿArabī mentions his encounter with one of the members of the 'Assembly of Saints' who immediately recommends that he associate with none of the spiritual masters he meets, "Associate only with God, for none of those whom you have met has authority over you; it is God Himself Who, in His Goodness, has taken you under His charge."[18]

There can be no better description of the independence of the 'solitary ones' who, Ibn ʿArabī emphasises, are all equal from the point of view of their *degree* of perfection. All of them have reached the 'station of proximity', which is located just below that of law-giving prophethood, which Ibn ʿArabī is not afraid to call the 'station of *general* prophethood'. Actually, the death of the Messenger of God forever sealed access to *law-giving* prophethood: no sacred law will come after his. But the *walāya*, that sainthood that emanates from the Muḥammadan Reality has not disappeared; it continues to shine in the person of the saints, and in its ultimate form, that of *general* prophethood, in the 'solitary ones'.

[18] *Fut.*, II, p. 573.

The Seal

THE MUḤAMMADAN HERITAGE that is transmitted to the 'solitary ones' is never totally complete. There is but one individual in the history of humanity who has received it in its entirety. It is upon this 'supreme heir of Muḥammad' that the privilege and the responsibility of wholly assuming *walāya* falls. It is this individual who is charged with the duty of being the unique, plenary manifestation of the 'hidden' face of the Prophet, the face of sainthood that his authority as prophet kept hidden. The death of this heir of the Prophet will definitively close *direct* access to Muḥammad's heritage; he is, consequently, the 'Seal of Muḥammadan Sainthood'. "As God has sealed legislative prophethood through Muḥammad, *through the Muḥammadan Seal he has sealed the sainthood which comes from the Muḥammadan heritage*, not the sainthood which comes from the heritage of the other prophets."[1] From that moment on, though there will still be 'solitary' individuals, they will not be able to inherit *directly* from Muḥammad.

The Shaykh al-Akbar, however, says that, "There is another Seal through whom God seals universal sainthood

[1] *Fut.*, II, p. 49, cited in Chodkiewicz, *Seal of the Saints*, p. 118.

from Adam up to the last of the saints, and that seal is Jesus. He is the Seal of Sainthood, just as he is also the Seal of the cycle of the Kingdom."[2] Elsewhere, Ibn ʿArabī is more precise, "When [Jesus] descends at the end of time, it will be as the Heir and the Seal, *and after him there will be no saint to be the holder of the prophethood in general.*"[3] The 'station of proximity' will thus be definitively taken from men when he is gone. Then the 'Seal of Children' will follow; he will be the last human born and the last saint to illumine the earth; "When God takes away his soul and that of the believers of his time, those who remain after him will be like beasts ... the only authority they will obey will be that of their animal natures ... and it is over them that the Hour will rise."[4]

Before we delve into a more detailed analysis of the idea of the Seal of Sainthood, let us remember that it was not Ibn ʿArabī who invented it. It can be traced back to the ninth century and to a Khurāsānī mystic, al-Ḥakīm Tirmidhī, whose most important work was precisely entitled *The Seal of Sainthood (Khatm al-walāya)*. And yet, it is not so much the question of the Seal that occupies the greater part of Tirmidhī's work, but the much broader question of *walāya*, for this was the first time that an author attempted to define its nature, its role, and its degrees. Ḥakīm Tirmidhī was also the first to risk—and this is the right word to use given the ill-treatment he suffered at the hands of the doctors of the Law—stating that, from *a certain point of view*, sainthood is superior to law-giving prophethood. The latter, he maintained, will lose its *raison d'être* at the end of the world, while *walāya*, sainthood, will eternally survive both in this world and the next. However, this does not mean that

[2] *Fut.*, II, p. 9.

[3] *Fut.*, II, p. 49, cited in Chodkiewicz, *Seal of the Saints*, p. 117.

[4] *Fuṣūṣ al-ḥikam* (hereafter *Fuṣūṣ*), ed. ʿAfīfī, Beirut, 1980, p. 67.

saints are superior to prophets, but only that in each of the prophets, sainthood is superior to the prophetic function. Tirmidhī referred to the Seal of Sainthood only in vague and allusive terms, and he remains silent as to the Seal's identity. But he does at least leave us with a message and a challenge: one hundred and fifty-seven abrupt, and often sibylline, questions the answers to which, he says, can only be given by the authentic Seal; no one would take up the challenge until Ibn ʿArabī.

Paradoxically, it was not in his 'Reply to Tirmidhī's Questions' (which takes up most of chapter 73 of the *Futūḥāt*) that the most explicit details of Ibn ʿArabī's teachings relative to the Seal are found; but in several other chapters of the *Futūḥāt* and in the second chapter of the *Fuṣūṣ*. We have seen that Ibn ʿArabī refers to three different Seals, and that he names Jesus as the one who fulfils the function of Seal of Universal Sainthood, thus considerably widening the eschatological role that Islam tends to ascribe to him. Ibn ʿArabī gives but one symbolic hint about the Seal of Children, and that is that he will be born "in China" and will come into the world after his twin sister. As to the identity of the Seal of Muḥammadan Sainthood, the author of the *Futūḥāt* claims to know who he is: he is an Arab of noble lineage living in Ibn ʿArabī's time. The name, which the Shaykh al-Akbar conceals both here and in all of his *prose* texts is revealed on a number of occasions in his *poetry*: it is his name. Here are two of a hundred different examples:

> I am the Seal of the Saints, just as it has been shown
> That the Seal of the Prophets is Muḥammad
> The specific Seal, not the Seal of General Sainthood,
> For that is Jesus, the Assisted One.[5]

[5] *Dīwān*, Būlāq, 1855, p. 293.

Or:

If I am neither Moses nor Jesus, nor their likes,
It is of no concern, since I am the sum of all of this,
For I am the Seal of the Saints of Muḥammad
The specific Seal in both cities and deserts.[6]

The question that comes immediately to mind is: why hide it here, but divulge it elsewhere? It appears as though the answer is to be found in the specific and all-important function that Ibn ʿArabī assigns to his poetry. Certain indications in the prologue to the *Collection of Divine Knowledge*—which contains, as we have seen, a number of priceless autobiographical details—suggest that, to his way of thinking, his poems, abstruse and enigmatic though they often were, were meant to be vehicles for the most esoteric aspects of his teaching.

It was in Cordoba, the same place where, as a young adolescent, he had suddenly made the choice to devote his life to God, that Ibn ʿArabī learned in a vision that he was destined to be the Seal of Muḥammadan Sainthood. Of the numerous texts that recount the event, the one found in the chapter of the *Fuṣūṣ* devoted to the prophet Hūd gives specific information relative to the place and the date. "Know that when God caused me to see and made me a witness of the meeting of all the prophets of the human race from Adam to Muḥammad, in a place in Cordoba where I was taken in the year 586 [1190], none of them addressed me except Hūd, who informed me of the reason for their gathering."[7] It is true that neither in this passage, nor in any of the other texts of which we are aware, does Ibn ʿArabī

[6] Ibid., p. 334.
[7] *Fuṣūṣ*, I, p. 110.

specifically say that Hūd revealed to him just then that he had been chosen to assume the supreme function of Muḥammadan Sainthood. But even if he did not write it, Ibn ᶜArabī did confide this detail to some of his disciples who passed on the information from generation to generation. Ṣadr al-Dīn Qūnawī—who, as we shall see, was raised by the Shaykh al-Akbar from a very early age—communicated it to his student Jandī, who reported it in his commentary on the *Fuṣūṣ*.

This first confirmation of the axial role that was to be his in the sphere of sainthood would be followed, throughout Ibn ᶜArabī's life, by other visionary events relative to his divine election. These were not, however, simple repetitions of the initial message: the vision in Cordoba announced his selection; those that followed gave additional information, sometimes about its nature, sometimes about its privileges, and sometimes about its duties.

"When what has never been disappears ..."

OF ALL HIS spiritual masters, the name that occurs most in the writing of the Shaykh al-Akbar is, paradoxically, a being that he never 'physically' met: Abū Madyan. Called 'Master of all masters' during his lifetime, this illustrious Andalusian saint has enjoyed tremendous popularity in the Maghreb throughout the centuries, and even up to the present day. It may be mentioned in passing, that his posthumous fate was in many ways analogous to Ibn ʿArabī's. Both individuals appear in a number of initiatory chains of Sufism, although neither one founded an autonomous brotherhood. As is the case with Ibn ʿArabī, Abū Madyan's teachings were widely known in the East as well as in the West, and his influence was felt both by erudite Sufism and by its popular tendencies.

Several of Ibn ʿArabī's Andalusian spiritual masters had been taught by Abū Madyan. This was particularly the case of Shaykh al-Kūmī, who never failed to praise the merits and virtues of the saint who resided in Bougie. Intrigued, Ibn ʿArabī ardently wished to meet Abū Madyan. But in 1190, Abū Madyan let him know that their meeting would not take place "in this world".[1] Three years later,

[1] Austin, *Sufis of Andalusia*, no. 19, p. 113.

Ibn ʿArabī abruptly decided to go to Tunis to meet with ʿAbd al-ʿAzīz al-Mahdawī (see box), one of the most famous disciples of Abū Madyan. If Abū Madyan had still been among the living, Ibn ʿArabī would undoubtedly have

The Sufi, the *faqīh* and the Christians

When [Shaykh ʿAbd al-ʿAzīz al-Mahdawī] departed for the pilgrimage with his companions, the enemy took them by surprise while crossing the sea, and a skirmish broke out between the two parties. The shaykh had been telling his companions about the essential truths and [in spite of what was happening] he did not stop what he was doing, and he continued to perform his usual devotions. Among the passengers was a doctor of the Law (*faqīh*) who was seized with fear and panic. He began to vilify the shaykh and criticise his attitude, "We are in the midst of a calamity, and about to succumb, but *he* is speaking about essential truths!" The shaykh did not pay him the slightest heed. A short while later, someone came to inform the shaykh that the enemy had taken control of the vessel, and that they were therefore prisoners. "So?" inquired the shaykh. "You are to board the Christians' ship, because we are now their captives." "Tell the Christians to save us a place to pray and to do our recitations." The Christians did just as they were asked—with God's permission, may he be praised!—and they honoured the shaykh and treated him with respect. But the recalcitrant doctor of the Law was the object of their scorn, and they struck him. The shaykh and his companions continued to be honoured; they were able to continue their devotions until they arrived safe and sound in a Muslim land.

Muḥammad al-Wazīr, *al-Ḥulal al-sundusiyya*

paid him a visit in Bougie. Thus the death of Abū Madyan—which some authors, most notably Ibn ʿArabī, place in 589 (1192-1193), while others give a later date—in all likelihood preceded his departure for the Maghreb.

Whatever may be the case, this was the first time that Ibn ʿArabī ventured out of Spain. The trip was to be of some consequence for the formation of his teachings and for his own spiritual journey. As we have seen, the Andalusian Sufis that Ibn ʿArabī frequented gave preference to the practice of the virtues over abstract teachings. Ibn ʿArabī would benefit from his stay in Tunis, where he remained in the company of Mahdawī for nearly a year, and were he was able to deepen his study of the great masters of Sufi thought. Most notably, he discovered the works of Ibn Barrajān (d. 1141), whose commentary on the Qur'ān he cited on a number of occasions. This Andalusian Sufi was a victim of Almoravid repression because of his claim to the imāmate. Ibn ʿArabī also met the son of Ibn Qaṣī, the head of the *murīdūn*, who had lead an insurrection against Almoravid power. At the end of the meeting, Ibn ʿArabī's judgement on the rebel from the Algarve was favourable. However, thirty years later, while undertaking a careful examination and commentary of his famous treatise, *The Removal of the Two Sandals*, Ibn ʿArabī's conclusion was that Ibn Qasī had been an impostor.

The relatively frequent allusions in Ibn ʿArabī's works to the religious theses expounded by his precursors show that Ibn ʿArabī both only carefully read these authors, and also borrowed a certain number of phrases from them. Nevertheless, the two main sources of inspiration for his teachings were the Qur'ān—we will be returning to this point—and his own experiences. From this point of view, his first sojourn in the Maghreb was of paramount importance. It was actually in Tunis, in 1194, that the Shaykh al-Akbar entered into the "God's Vast Land".

The 'Imaginal World', Land of Contemplation

There are two autobiographical accounts[2] that give detailed descriptions of this event. He was praying behind an imām, when the imām came to the verse, "O my servants! My land is vast, so worship me."[3] In rapture, Ibn ᶜArabī cried out such that everyone present fainted. This was the only time during his spiritual journey, as he later told his disciple Ibn Sawdakīn, that he happened to cry out in such a way.

Ibn ᶜArabī wrote a "large book" about this 'Land of God', which he also referred to as the 'Land of Reality' (*arḍ al-ḥaqīqa*); unfortunately, it has not survived. But chapter eight of the *Futūḥāt* is entirely devoted to the subject. Created from the clay left over from Adam, the 'Land of Reality' consists of the 'imaginal world'; it is the isthmus that links the image of the Perfect Man with all the orders of reality, be they lesser or greater, divine or belonging to the creatures. A supernatural hand where everything is not only incorruptible, but lives and speaks; a spiritual hand where bodies are composed of subtle matter, while the intelligibles are clothed with form: this is why "the gnostics enter it only by the spirit and leave their corporal envelopes in the lesser world". And finally, as a land of contemplation, it is the theatre where all the visions of the contemplatives are played out, where dreams take place, and where the souls waiting the Last Judgment reside.

[2] *Fut.*, I, p. 173; *K. al-Tajalliyāt*, Tehran, 1988, p. 454.
[3] Qur'ān 29:56.

This idea of the 'imaginal world' is not just Ibn ʿArabī's; it is also to be found in Shīʿite gnosis, and has been extensively studied by Henri Corbin.[4] Corbin's excellent publications have unquestionably contributed to a better understanding of Ibn ʿArabī's thought in Europe. And yet, it is also important to note that the great Iranologist, who based his ideas on an incomplete knowledge of Ibn ʿArabī's texts, was unaware of some of the ideas on which the concept of the 'imaginal world' was based. Moreover, he overestimated the role that Ibn ʿArabī assigned to this world.

In a section of chapter 351 of the *Futūḥāt* entitled 'servitude', Ibn ʿArabī states, "No one fully assumes servitude unless he lives in the 'Vast Land of God' which contains the eternal and the contingent. This Land is so constructed that he who lives in it attains to the pure worship that God is due. I myself began to worship God in it in 590 [1193] and we are now in 635 [1237]."[5] From what he goes on to say, the very nature of this Land is to be the recipient of absolute divine sovereignty. This crushing theophany, pulverises the contemplative's consciousness of his original theomorphism. From that moment on, he has direct, unmitigated perception of his ontological servitude. Which is why, he who penetrates into the 'Vast Land of God' is destined to remain there forever. Citing a saying of the Prophet which states that "there is no exile after the conquest", Ibn ʿArabī declares, "He whom God has illuminated sees Him in all things."[6] God is thus never absent from such a person;

[4] Corbin, *Creative Imagination in the Sufism of Ibn ʿArabī*, Princeton, Princeton University Press, 1969; and *Spiritual Body and Celestial Earth*, Princeton, Princeton University Press, 1977.

[5] *Fut.*, III, p. 224.

[6] *Fut.*, III, p. 247.

wherever the person may be, he remains in the 'Land of God'.

The Supreme Vision

Given the above, one may be tempted to conclude, as was the case with Corbin, that the 'imaginal world' offers man the highest degree of contemplation of the Divine Being. However, it is an imperfect contemplation. Regardless of how sublime it may appear to be, a theophany in imaginal form is no less *formal*, and consequently cannot reflect the Uncreated. A comment, which Ibn ʿArabī' inserts in chapter 351 of the *Futūḥāt*, nevertheless demonstrates that Ibn ʿArabī did not exclude the possibility of formless theophanies revealing the Divine Essence in its Absolute Simplicity, beyond any form or image. "The only reason the intelligibles take on a form is because of the inability of certain minds to apprehend that which has no form. But those gnostics who are anchored in the knowledge of God do not perceive the intelligibles in forms, nor do they perceive forms other than as they are. They apprehend each thing according to the nature that is proper to it, whatever it may be." Another comment from chapter 8 of the *Futūḥāt* and partially translated by Corbin, should have aroused his suspicion. In it, Ibn ʿArabī states that the theophanies of the 'imaginal world' can be thus described: that they do not tear the gnostic away from himself, with the result that he remains conscious of his being. On the other hand, the other theophanies "enrapture him and extinguish his contemplation, whether he be one of the prophets or one of the saints". Elsewhere he affirms that this is eminently the case with the *informal* theophanies.[7]

[7] *Fut.*, III, p. 107.

The gap between the 'permanence' of the gnostic who is aware of himself (*baqā'*) and the 'extinction' (*fanā'*) of the one whose contemplation has enraptured him, is as great as that between day and night. The adventitious cannot contain the Uncreated. Aware of himself when the theophanies occur in the imaginal mode, the contemplative can, according to Ibn ʿArabī, at the same time both see and understand God; but we are here referring to *formal*, and thus created, theophanies, theophanies that are conditioned and that have no common measure with Divine Infinitude. Only the Eternal can contemplate the Eternal. In *The Book of Extinction*, Ibn ʿArabī states, "As long as a trace of the creature remains in the eye of the contemplator, the Divine Reality will remain too elevated for this eye to contemplate." The *formless* theophanies, which reveal the completely unveiled Essence, demand the extinction of the creature who is unaware of seeing God at the very moment that he sees Him, since he does not know that he is. Only after he comes back to himself does the contemplative enjoy, *a posteriori*, the ineffable joy that is granted by this dazzling manifestation of the Divine Being.

We should not deduce from the above that the fully assumed 'servitude' that leads the saint into the 'Vast Land of God' would be a useless detour for Ibn ʿArabī. On the contrary, it is the only road that can lead man to that 'night' of his being where he can contemplate the One that has no second. Another chapter from the *Futūḥāt*, entitled 'On the knowledge of the abode of paths and of the vast land of God ...'[8], adds equally valuable information regarding this point, especially since here Ibn ʿArabī not only mentions the goal that is to be attained, but also explains the means by

[8] *Fut.*, III, pp. 247-252.

which this goal can be reached. "Know, my brother, that the land of your body where He has commanded you to worship Him, is the true 'Vast Land of God'; for He has commanded you to worship him on His land only for as long as your spirit abides within your body; from the moment that it leaves your body you are no longer under any legal obligation."

Mandated on earth to perform 'service to God' (*ʿibāda*), man was created of earth, and it is to the earth that his body will return, because the earth is humble by its very essence. That is why, according to Ibn ʿArabī, God has 'shortened' the route that is to lead man back to his origins, back to his ontological servitude. If he humbly and strictly gives in to those obligations that God has prescribed for him, and he makes his body into the place where his servitude is to take place, he will be able to contemplate his Sovereign at every single moment. But he who knows himself to be a servant is still conscious of a [separate] existence; consequently, he thinks of himself as being distinct from the Divine Being Who, from that moment on, cannot manifest Himself to him in His plenitude. "He who sees Me and knows that he sees Me, does not see Me";[9] this is the indefeasible divine rule. Supreme knowledge of God, paradoxically, implies the most absolute ignorance, and the vision of His Essence does not take place, in the words of a famous saying often quoted by Ibn ʿArabī, except "when what has never been disappears, and what has never ceased to be, remains". It is thus reserved for him who, having plunged into the night of his original nothingness, no longer knows that he is.

Ibn ʿArabī's journey to Tunis opened a new chapter in his odyssey. It began the *siyāḥa*: the long period of 'wandering'

[9] *Fut.*, IV, p. 55.

through *dār al-islām*, the Muslim world, which would last some thirty years. A vision that took place just as he was preparing to cross the Strait of Gibraltar for the first time underscores the importance of this passing from a 'sedentary' life to a 'nomadic' life. Thanks to this vision, Ibn ᶜArabī knew what his fate would be and what would be the fate of his future disciples. Armed with this certainty, he began to wander the earth of men. And suddenly, he departed forever into the 'Vast Land of God'. Plunged into contemplation of the "Supreme Companion", he learned that he was the "heir of Muḥammad's knowledge". At about the same time, another visionary event appears to have taken place: it revealed to him that his teaching was destined to spread over "the two horizons, that of the West and that of the East". Aged then about thirty, Ibn ᶜArabī would devote the remainder of his life to the transmission, both orally and in writing, of the precious legacy that had been consigned to him.

"The distance of two bows, or closer"

IN 1194, NEARLY a year after he left, Ibn ʿArabī returned to Andalusia. The truce signed with the Castillians four years earlier had expired, and Alphonse VIII's troops were sacking Seville and its surroundings. In Marrakesh, the caliph was calling his troops to arms. Personal trials were piled on top of these exterior difficulties. Shortly after his return, Ibn ʿArabī lost his father.[1] Apparently, this death was followed a short time later by that of his mother. Since he was the only male child, Ibn ʿArabī was now responsible for his two sisters. It was urgently impressed upon him by members of his entourage that, his devotion to God, was incompatible with his new responsibilities as the head of a family: he must take up a profitable position of some sort, as was his birthright. But in vain. Now an adult, Ibn ʿArabī did not have the least intention of deviating even an iota from the course that he had set out on as an adolescent. Moreover, he began to write, and to write profusely. Contemplating God was not enough; he was calling Him.

Soon after his return, he completed a work which he significantly entitled *The Book of Contemplations of Sublime*

[1] On this subject, see Addas, *Quest for the Red Sulphur*, pp. 122-123.

Secrets (*Kitāb mashāhid al-asrār al-qudsiyya*). According to what he tells us, the book was intended for the 'heirs'; it was evidently the fruit of his recent experiences in the 'imaginal world'. Moreover, Ibn ʿArabī maintained from the outset that God had enjoined him to "make this book manifest in the '*sensible world*'". Its rich, and dense introduction deals essentially, albeit convolutedly, with the idea of 'prophetic inheritance'. At this early stage, we already find those themes that were to become foundational in Ibn ʿArabī's hagiology, and that would later be amply developed in the *Futūḥāt*: for example, the differentiation between saints that have definitively 'stopped' in the Divine Presence (*wāqifūn*) and those who come back toward creatures in order to give them guidance (*rāji'ūn*). The introduction is followed by fourteen 'contemplations', face-to-face encounters between the creature and his Creator. The Creator reminds man of his initial vocation of a 'Perfect Man' (*insān kāmil*) through which he is God's viceregent, "You are My Names, the sign of My Essence ... He who sees you, sees Me. He who honours you, honours Me. He who treats you with spite treats himself with spite. He who humiliates you humiliates himself. You are My mirror, My house, My dwelling place; you are the treasure of My mystery, the place of My knowledge. If you had never been, I would not be known, worshipped, thanked, or denied ..."[2]

The Perfect Man is again the subject of the *Divine Ordonnances* (*al-Tadbīrāt al-ilāhiyya*), a work composed shortly before, or shortly after, the *Contemplations*. The exact chronology of the writings dating from the Western

[2] *Kitāb mashāhid al-asrār al-qudsiyya*, edited from the Arabic and translated into Spanish by S. Ḥakīm and P. Beneito, Murcia, 1994, pp. 58-59 of the Arabic text.

period of Ibn ʿArabī's life remains uncertain. The *Divine Ordonnances* is actually mentioned twice in the *Contemplations*, but that proves nothing. Close examination of the texts suggests that Ibn ʿArabī frequently 'retouched' works he had composed earlier. This is true both of those works whose composition spread over a long period and of those written 'in one fell swoop'. There is thus no way of knowing which of these two works of his youth predates the other, nor what their dates of composition are. On the other hand, it is certain that the period following his return from Tunis is the one during which his literary genius began to unfold at an increasing speed.

As we mentioned above, the central theme in both the *Contemplations* and the *Divine Ordonnances* is the same. However, both the style and the approach radically differ. The *Contemplations* is the work of a visionary: the writing is evanescent and inflected, imbuing the work with a lyric, perhaps even poetic, quality. But the *Divine Ordonnances*—which Ibn ʿArabī tells us he composed in four days in the Andalusian city of Morón—is slow, discursive prose, the meticulous and detailed arguments of a teacher. The *Contemplations* is the exaltation of theomorphic man; the *Ordonnances* is a didactic exposé on the role that the intellect, the body, the soul, and the senses, play in restoring the aspirant, effectively and not only virtually, to his original theomorphism, to the Perfect Man who combines in his person all the orders of divine and creatural realities. The mention, in this text, of six other works is evidence of the intense pace of Ibn ʿArabī's literary production during this period. These six books are considered to be writings of his youth, although it is not possible to affirm categorically that they were composed before the *Ordonnances*.

Paradoxically, this fever of writing occurred at a time

when conditions were less than favourable for writing. Eager to escape the pressure of his relations, Ibn ᶜArabī was frequently on the move and in a country preparing for war. He was in Fez when, in June 1195, Manṣūr and his army arrived in Seville, ready for the great battle that was about to be waged. The confrontation was a decisive one, as we know. But was it to be favourable to the Muslims, or to the Christians? Ibn ᶜArabī claims to have had no doubt that the outcome of the battle would be favourable.[3] He had barely arrived back in Seville when the Almohads, on 18 July 1195, crushed the Christians at the battle of Alarcos. The Andalusians were elated, unaware that the victory they were celebrating was the swan song of Muslim Spain. However, they did have a few good days still before them. And as proof of this, Manṣūr lead his army to Toledo. But this was less a victory march than a military parade hopeful of banishing fate, or hopeful of persuading the enemy (and even more so of persuading the Muslims themselves) that Muslim Spain was indestructible. At least for the time being, the Christians ceased their raids on the Sevillian countryside.

The pressure to bring Ibn ᶜArabī back to a life of worldly concerns was becoming daily more intense. Finally, the caliph intervened personally: he summoned Ibn ᶜArabī and implored him to leave to him the responsibility of finding suitable husbands for his sisters. The young shaykh firmly but courteously refused. And in order to escape any further approaches, he packed his bags and took his sisters to Fez.[4]

His first brief visit to Fez two years earlier had given Ibn ᶜArabī the opportunity to find his bearings and to make

[3] *Fut.*, IV, p. 220.

[4] Austin, *Sufis of Andalusia*, no. 3, pp. 65-66.

contacts. Like him, a number of Sufis had chosen to take up residence in the Moroccan metropolis, where the environment was favourable to spiritual life. A small circle of followers soon gathered around the young master. Most notable among these was the radiant countenance of an emancipated slave, Badr al-Ḥabashī. A number of Ibn ᶜArabī's poems praise the virtues and the holiness of his Ethiopian companion. A faithful disciple, and an even more devoted friend, Ḥabashī would follow his master wherever he went: Morocco, Spain, Algeria, Tunisia, the Arabian Peninsula, Palestine, Mesopotamia, and finally Anatolia, where death was to separate them in 1221.

The 'Nocturnal Voyage'

In Fez, Ibn ᶜArabī undoubtedly found the solace he was seeking. He remained in the city for two years and it was there that, in the month of March 1198, he finished one of his most beautiful—and one of his most difficult—works, the *Book of the Nocturnal Journey* (*Kitāb al-isrā'*). In the Islamic tradition, the word *isrā'*, 'nocturnal journey', recalls the night in the life of the Prophet when he was miraculously transported from Mecca to Jerusalem, and from Jerusalem to the Divine Throne. This celestial pilgrimage—which, from heaven to heaven, led him into the presence of God, to "the distance of two bows, or closer"[5]—was not, to Ibn ᶜArabī's mind, a possibility reserved exclusively for the Prophet. The same experience is open to his 'heirs', with the one difference being that in the Prophet's case the ascension took place in body, while the saints can experience it in spirit only. A vertical journey, but a nocturnal one: it is only after he has taken refuge in the

[5] Qur'ān 53:9.

night of his ontological indigence that the contemplative can encounter the One Who has no second.

Ibn ʿArabī addresses this theme of the 'nocturnal journey' on a number of occasions. Aside from the *Epistle of Light*, which he composed in Konya in 1205, he dedicates to it two long chapters of the *Futūḥāt*. Chapter 167 is presented in allegorical form, while chapter 367, like the *Nocturnal Journey*, is a first person account of his own ascension. But the two books differ in more than one way. In the *Futūḥāt*, the narration is linear, the prose is sober and polished. The *Nocturnal Journey*, which is in the same vein as the *Contemplations*, has a much stronger poetic resonance: the text is in rhymed prose interspersed with poems, and astonishingly rich in symbolism. Entranced by the incantatory power of the poetic rhyme, intoxicated by the echo of the rhythm, the reader feels almost projected out of the empirical world. The *Book of the Nocturnal Journey* undoubtedly deserves a place among the masterpieces of Arabic literature.

From the dazzling experience of his 'nocturnal journey', Ibn ʿArabī drew at least two firm conclusions. The first of these concerned the position of great authority that was assigned to him in the hierarchy of sainthood. Throughout his ascension, the prophets he met received him in terms that explicitly confirmed his having been named as 'Seal of Sainthood'. The second conclusion was that his role required that he make his way from the periphery of the Muslim world to its centre and that he set up residence there.

Farewell to the West

After a certain time in the Maghreb, Ibn ʿArabī returned to Andalusia accompanied by al-Ḥabashī. It was then that a long pilgrimage began, a pilgrimage of farewell which he described in a letter to a friend, probably al-Mahdawī, with a certain amount of melancholy. Algeciras, Ronda, Seville: at each stop Ibn ʿArabī bid adieu to those who had been the first witnesses to his quest. In December 1198, he was in Cordoba, where he followed Averroes's funeral procession. It was perhaps in this city ("a place of sublime contemplations", as he wrote to his friend) that a few weeks later, in January 1199, he experienced a visionary event that gave rise to an enigmatic work: *The Astonishing Phoenix, on the Seal of Saints and the Sun of the West* (*Kitāb ʿAnqā' al-mughrib fī khatm al-awliya' wa-shams al-maghrib*). Eschatological details about the coming of Jesus, the Seal of Universal Sainthood, and the Mahdī, are scattered throughout the book in a language purposefully coded. The precaution was necessary under a regime that based its legitimacy on Ibn Tumert's claim to be the 'Impeccable Imām' awaited by Muslims at the end of time. The Almohad dynasty had little appreciation, to say the least, for anything having even the closest resemblance to millenarianism.

After a stop in Granada, it was in his native city of Murcia that Ibn ʿArabī ended his farewell tour. At the end of his letter, he wrote, "From this point on I will visit no one else, no matter how long I stay." And for the next year and a half we lose all trace of the Shaykh al-Akbar. His works, which are usually so rich in autobiographical details, are completely silent on this period. One thing is certain: in July 1199, he composed (in a period of eleven days) *The Setting of the Stars* (*Mawāqi' al-nujūm*). This extremely dense work deals with the relationship between the legal prescriptions to which different parts of the body are subjected, and the blessings that result from them.

The following year, Ibn ʿArabī crossed the Strait of Gibraltar for the last time. In October, we find him in Salé, where he bids farewell to Shaykh al-Kūmī before continuing his journey towards Marrakesh. At the half-way point, he stopped in a small Berber village, still in existence today, called Guisser. An important spiritual event took place there, the event that marked his accession to the 'station of proximity', the spiritual abode reserved for the 'solitary ones'. After stopping in Marrakesh, and then in Fez, he turned north again. In June 1201, he was in Bougie when, in a dazzling vision, he saw the celebration of his marriage to each of the stars in the sky and to each of the letters of the alphabet. This event, like the one that preceded it in Guisser, confirmed in his eyes his election as Seal of Muḥammadan Sainthood. If the first of these events falls under the jurisdiction of the spiritual degree that this function implies, the second refers, evidently, to Islam's sacred esoteric sciences of astrology and the 'science of letters' (*ʿilm al-ḥurūf*), of which the Seal is both the guardian and the repository.

Continuing his itinerary along the coast, Ibn ʿArabī finally reached Tunis, where with Ḥabashī he stayed at the home of Shaykh Mahdawī. Nine months later he resumes his travels, with his destination set on Mecca. The sadness that pervades the epistle in which he describes his systematic leave–takings of the places and persons who had shared his life, leaves no doubt that he knew that his was a journey of no return. But had he refused to go, he would not have been able to fully assume the function that was destined to be his, the importance and extent of which required his expatriation toward the cradle of Muḥammad's revelations. Moreover, he could not have been unaware of the fact that the Muslim kingdom of Spain was doomed to disappear sooner or later. A number of Andalusians experienced quite early on what Maribel Fierro calls the 'feeling of precariousness', that painful intuition that, sooner or later, the Christians would end up prevailing over them.

However, nothing, or almost nothing, seemed to justify such pessimism at the time. Manṣūr's kingdom brought the Almohad empire to its apogee. His military successes and the solid administration with which he endowed the country appeared enough to assure the stability of the regime. In the field of art, he gloriously continued the work begun by his father. Under his aegis, monuments that are among the masterpieces of Hispano-Mauresque civilisation were constructed; among these, the Giralda de Sevilla, the Kutubiyya in Marrakesh, the Tower of Ḥasan in Rabāṭ. Intelligent and cultured, he was, like his father, an enlightened Maecenas. The support that father and son gave to men like Ibn Ṭufayl, the author of the great philosophical novel *The Living Son of the Vigilant*, and to Averroes, to Ibn Zuhr (the Latin Avenzoar, whose medical manual was translated into Latin in the thirteenth century), and to Biṭrūjī (Alpetragius, whose treatise on astronomy Michael Scot translated in 1217), made the flowering of scientific and philosophical production possible, an event whose lasting influence on Latin Europe is of course well known. But the Reconquista was still gaining ground. Thirteen years after Manṣūr's death the bitter defeat of Las Navas de Tolosa took place, and with it, the slow agony of Muslim Spain.

The Meccan Illuminations

"THE FATHER HAS died ... his sons and brother will follow the example he set."[1] Such was the message that Saladin's eldest son, Afḍal, hurriedly dispatched to Caliph Naṣīr when the conqueror of Hattin passed away in March 1193. But was the commitment to follow the founder of the Ayyūbid state really respected by his successors? As Saladin's son wrote, the state was based on three great principles: orthodoxy, holy war and obedience to the caliph. Historians concur that the first and third principles were adhered to. The construction of a number of schools of religious teaching (*madrasa*), and the political role that certain great *ʿūlamā'* played as 'counsellors to the prince' bear witness to, among other things, the willingness of the Ayyūbid sovereigns to be vigilant guardians of Sunnī Islam. The signs of deference that they abundantly showed to the caliph of Baghdad were also in line with Saladin's ideology. Faithful vassals of the ʿAbbāsid Empire—or at least trying to appear so—they intended to ask the caliph to legitimising their territorial sovereignty. Several of the Ayyūbids, moreover, belonged to the *futuwwa*, a far-reaching circle

[1] Cf. E. Sivan, *L'Islam et la Croisade*, Paris, Adrien Maisonneuve, 1968, p. 133.

organised by caliph Naṣīr with the help of a great Baghdad Sufi, Suhrawardī (d. 1234), with the goal of gathering together the Muslim princes together under the standard of the Caliphate.

But, as to the pursuit of *jihād*, the holy war against the Franks whom Saladin had chased out of Jerusalem in 1187, one has to admit that his heirs were rather more reticent. Family squabbles had set one against the other, and concerns about replenishing the state treasury, which Saladin had left depleted, persuaded them to look for a *modus vivendi* with the Franks. At times, this policy of 'peaceful coexistence', which would ultimately lead them to return the cities conquered by Richard the Lion-Heart's illustrious adversary, elicited hostile reactions within the heart of the population, specifically in Damascus. Nor did this policy put an end to new crusades; the cycle of *Gesta Dei per Francos* was not yet over.

The Reconquista continued to provoke waves of Andalusian emigrants toward the countries of the Levant. Thus Ibn ʿArabī encountered a number of his compatriots, first upon his arrival in Egypt, and later throughout his wanderings in the East. Although some of these did return to Andalusia once their pilgrimage was accomplished, others like Ibn ʿArabī, chose to take up permanent residence in the East. The hospitable Ayyūbid princes took pains to make the settlement of these immigrants, including the Sufis, easier. Thanks to Saladin, the Sufis had at their disposal a large convent (*khāniqa*) in Cairo. This act of kindness was certainly not entirely devoid of political astuteness; in gathering them together in a structured organisation and placing them under the authority of a hierarchical superior (the *shaykh al-shuyūkh* was chosen by the Sultan) the Ayyūbids gave themselves a means by which they could control these sometimes suspect dervishes from faraway lands.

Having arrived in Cairo, Ibn ʿArabī made his way to the famous convent, "hoping to find there the breath of the Supreme Companion". His disappointment was immense; "I was led to a group assembled in a *khāniqa* located in a grand and spacious building; I noticed that their greatest concern and their primary preoccupation was cleaning their frocks—or should I say their uniforms?—and combing their beards ..."[2] As far as we can tell, Ibn ʿArabī had no appreciation for this kind of organised, communitary mysticism, a mysticism so different from the fluid spiritual universe, completely devoid of decorum, that he knew in the West. Certainly, there were authentic saints living in the shadows of these prestigious convents in the East. The Shaykh al-Akbar, who had met more than one of them—most notably in Mecca, where he wrote the above lines taken from the *Epistle on the Spirit of Sainthood (Rūḥ al-quds)*—was as aware of this as anyone. But he was also aware that, as ineluctable as it was, the institutionalisation of Sufism—its development and its spread—was the harbinger of spiritual impoverishment. To his mind, the search for God was the silent journey of a soul in search of the Divine Presence in the most secret part of itself.

"Here I am, Lord, all Yours"

Ibn ʿArabī spent little time in plague infested and famine-stricken Egypt. In 1202, after passing the month of Ramaḍān in Cairo, he journeyed to Palestine and, from Jerusalem, he made his way toward the holy places. The day had finally arrived when he was able to raise his voice in the

[2] *Rūḥ*, pp. 21, 26.

chant of the pilgrims on their march to the 'House of God', "Here I am, Lord, all yours, here I am!" His voice joined the voices of thousands of men and women. From every direction they were converging on the 'Mother of Cities', Mecca. Shoulder to shoulder, they revolved slowly around the Kaᶜba, celebrating the praise of the One God in a resounding murmur. Like so many others before them, they had heard the message of Abraham who, in ages past, had called all men to come and make the pilgrimage.[3] The cubic sanctuary veiled in black, the Kaᶜba, built by Abraham and his son had been destroyed and rebuilt a number of times. The angular stone that, according to Islamic tradition, had been brought down from Paradise by Gabriel is still there today, blackened, it is said, by the sins of humanity. It was near this Black Stone, where the pilgrim begins and ends his circumambulations of the Kaᶜba, that Ibn ᶜArabī caught sight of the *fatā*, the 'Young Man'.

Before embarking upon the story of their encounter, let us state that Ibn ᶜArabī had already happened upon this mysterious character in the West, and apparently on a number of occasions. One poem in the *Dīwān* notably recalls an encounter that took place in Andalusia, thus long before the encounter in Mecca.[4]

The description of this silent *fatā* which is to be found in the text of the *Futūḥāt* that refers to the Meccan encounter is analogous to those found elsewhere and make it impossible to think that they refer to a different person. he also appears at the beginning of the *Book of the Nocturnal Journey*, where he is Ibn ᶜArabī's 'initiator', *stricto sensu*, on the long quest of his 'night journey'.

[3] Qur'ān 22:27.

[4] *Dīwān*, p. 384.

The text of the *Futūḥāt*, however, offers additional information about his nature and function, "While I was completing the circumambulations ... just as I found myself in front of the Black Stone, I encountered the radiant young man, the silent interlocutor, he-who-is-neither-living-nor-dead, he who is simple and complex, he who is enveloped and envelopes [...] Then God had me know the dignity of this young man and his transcendence in relation to 'where' and 'why'. When I understood his dignity and his lineage, when I saw his rank in existence and his state, I kissed his right hand, I wiped the perspiration of revelation from his forehead and I stated, 'Look upon him who aspires to your company and longs for your intimacy!' He answered me, by signs and enigmas, that he had been created in such a manner that he never spoke except by symbols. [...] He made a gesture, and I understood. The reality of his beauty was unveiled for me and I was overwhelmed by love. I was drained of strength, and instantly fell to the ground. When I regained consciousness, my ribs still quaking with fear, he knew that I had understood who he was. [...] He said, 'Take note of the details of my composition and the arrangement of my form! [...] I am Knowledge, the Known, and the Knower, I am Sapience, the Sapiential Work, and the Sage, [...] I am the mature orchard and the total harvest! Now lift up my veils, and read what my inscriptions contain. What you see in me, put down in your book and preach it to all your friends.'"[5] And thus, *The Meccan Illuminations* came to be.[6] From the very being of the Young Man, this paradoxical epiphany of 'Him Who

[5] *Fut.*, I, pp. 47-51; our translation is largely taken from an unpublished article by Michel Vâlsan.

[6] On this subject, cf. M. Chodkiewicz, *An Ocean Without Shore*, Albany, SUNY Press, 1995, pp. 28, 79, 96-97, 98.

speaks' (*al-Mutakallim*) but whose Word is beyond sounds, Ibn ᶜArabī took the contents of this *Summa Mystica* which has nourished generations of spiritual Muslims from the East and the West, from Asia and Africa. It is clearly of some import that this event, which was so decisive for the spiritual future of the *umma*—the Muḥammadan community which, according to Ibn ᶜArabī, includes all of humanity—should have taken place in Mecca, the 'navel of the Earth' according to traditional Arabic geography, and near the Kaᶜba, the 'heart of the universe'. In the *Futūḥāt* the placing of this event before the five hundred and sixty chapters that make up the work, is also every bit as significant.

Just as the earlier interventions of the *fatā* prepared the pilgrim for the *Meccan Illuminations*, the different visionary events that marked the stages of his search in the West appear like so many preparatory steps to his investiture as the 'Muḥammadan Seal'. Not surprisingly, this investiture took place upon his arrival in Mecca. The detailed description of the event, which marked his effective assumption of his spiritual role, appears in the prologue to the *Futūḥāt*[7] and implies that the person of Ibn ᶜArabī too was intimately linked with the creation of this work. Born from the silent revelations of the *fatā* whose interpreter (*tarjumān*) Ibn ᶜArabī was, the *Futūḥāt* were also the testament of the Seal of the Saints.

Ibn ᶜArabī arrived in Mecca at the end of 598 AH (August 1202), the pilgrimage month corresponding to the last month of the Muslim lunar calendar. Some three weeks later, the arrival of 599, the year that brought to a close the sixth century after the *hijra*, was accompanied by a wind of

[7] Cf. Chodkiewicz *Seal of the Saints*, pp. 131f.

cinders that plunged the Yemen into darkness, and by a shower of comets that danced in the eastern skies. "I was finishing the ritual circumambulations," Ibn ʿArabī recounts, "when I, and the rest of those who were circumambulating around the Kaʿba, noticed them. People were stunned; never had anyone seen a night with so many comets. They lasted throughout the night until the break of day. There were so many of them that they bumped into each other like sparks from a fire and the stars could no longer be seen. When we saw this, we said to each other that it must be a herald of an event of some gravity ..."[8] The Reconquista in the West, the Franks in the East, the Turks sweeping through Iran; there was no need to be a prophet to predict dark days for the Muslims. Caliph Nāṣir had a premonition of what was coming and attempted to stir up the conscience of the princes to restore the unity of the *umma*. But the die had been cast. The cataclysm was soon to arrive from the far reaches of the Asiatic steppes: the Mongol hordes would wipe out the caliphate in 1258.

Borders were changing, sacred institutions were caving in, *dār al-islām* was staggering. Ever since the death of the 'master of lovers', the Prophet, spiritual adepts had been orally passing on the heritage of wisdom. It was now time for this 'sacred repository' to be consigned to writing. That is just what Ibn ʿArabi undertook when composing the *Futūḥāt*: the preservation, beyond the vicissitudes of history, of the 'sacred repository' and its transmission to the generations of the future. The *Futūḥāt* are certainly an impressive synthesis that embraces all the spiritual sciences and that brings order to the doctrinal heritage of spiritual teachers of both East and West. But the *Futūḥāt* were much

[8] *Fut.*, II, p. 450.

more than an encyclopedic compendium of esoteric Islam. The duty of the Seal, which the author of the work had taken upon himself, was not solely to preserve the 'sacred repository'; it was also to *revivify* it. Thus, Ibn ʿArabī was not content to just codify existing terminology by both defining and expanding upon the meaning of the technical terms in usage. He considerably enriched this terminology by drawing upon the language of the Qur'ān and of the Prophetic traditions. *Nafas raḥmānī*, 'merciful breath', *fayḍ aqdas*, 'most holy flow', *khalq jadīd*, 'renewed creation' ... are all terms that would soon find their way into the *lingua franca* of the 'men of God' (*ahl Allāh*) and that would enter into such current usage that they would also show up, quite ironically, in the writings of those opposed to the school of Ibn ʿArabī.

We have already come across some of Ibn ʿArabī's texts that deal with the doctrinal themes of his hagiography and which are based on this vocabulary. We have also seen that even though the idea of *walāya* appears very early on in Sufism, it is Ibn ʿArabī who was the first person to exhaustively interpret its nature, its function and its types. We will now see that the same observations can be applied to the Shaykh al-Akbar's ontological and metaphysical teachings.

"God is, and nothing is with Him"

"NOTHING COMES TO You from anyone; nothing comes from You to anyone; everything comes from You to You, You are everything, and that is all."[1] Ibn ʿArabī was not the author of these lines which so forcefully express the primary principle of his metaphysical doctrine. They were penned by Shaykh Anṣārī, a well-known Khurāsānī Sufi who died in 1089, long before Ibn ʿArabī's birth. Thus, the idea of *waḥdat al-wujūd*, of 'the oneness of Being'—and we shall soon return to the origin of this famous expression—did not suddenly appear in the thirteenth century. If it was never explicitly formulated before the time of the Shaykh al-Akbar, it was nonetheless present, in germinal form, in the metaphysical teachings of a number of spiritual masters who preceded him. It is interesting to note that on several occasions Ibn ʿArabī comments on a famous sentence by this same Shaykh Anṣārī (although he attributed it to Ibn al-ʿArīf, who used it in his *Beauties of Spiritual Sessions*), "When what has never been disappears and what has never ceased to be remains..." If, from the

[1] From Anṣārī's *Munājāt*; see the article by S. de Beaurecueil, "Mémoire de l'homme ou mémoire de Dieu," *MIDEO*, 22, 1994, pp. 73-94.

point of view of spiritual realisation, this saying shows the degree of perfection of the 'pure servant' who, engulfed in the Deity, no longer knows that he is, from a metaphysical point of view, it illustrates the idea that 'existing beings' (*mawjūdāt*) have no being of their own, that *wujūd*, 'Being', belongs only to God.

Built on the rich (in possible meanings) root *wjd*, whose original meaning is 'to find', the word *wujūd* (corresponding in English to the passive infinitive of the verb to find 'to be found', thus, 'to be there') appears in Islamic philosophy in al-Fārābī (d. 950), with the meaning 'being' (*actus essendi*). This is the meaning that it has in the expression *waḥdat al-wujūd*, which, although never used by Ibn ʿArabī, adequately defines the fundamental theme of his doctrine, that of 'the unicity of Being'. Thus, it is preferable to avoid the frequent use (as in Izutsu, for example) of 'unicity of existence'; the word 'existence' implying, etymologically, a relationship to an origin and is thus appropriate, properly speaking, only in reference to what is 'outside God'. Nevertheless, it must be admitted that Ibn ʿArabī himself occasionally uses *wujūd* where he would be expected to use *mawjūd* ('existing being') or its plural *mawjūdāt* (the totality of 'existing beings', the universe). Thus, it is only careful reading that allows one to escape the pitfalls of amphibology.

Ibn ʿArabī was not a philosopher; his knowledge of philosophy, be it Greek or Arab, does not appear to surpass that which any cultured individual of his time might have gleaned, for example, from the writings of al-Ghazālī. If he criticised the philosophers in his work *The Incoherence of the Philosophers* (*Tahāfut al-falāsifa*), al-Ghazālī begins by exposing their theses in *The Goals of the Philosophers* (*Maqāṣid al-falāsifa*). But if the practice of this cultural *lingua franca* allows Ibn ʿArabī to use a conceptual language that is relatively easy to translate (it is also the language of medieval Christian scholasticism), his work bears witness to a preference for symbolic vocabulary borrowed from the Qur'ān and the *ḥadīth*. In other words, if he occasionally speaks of *hayūlā* (the *hylé* of Greek philosophy) to name the *materia prima*, he prefers to call it *al-habā'*, 'the dust', a word that he borrows from the Prophet. Likewise, when it comes to two terms that are equivalent in his writings, those of *al-ʿaql awwal* (first intellect) and *al-qalam* ('calamus'), he tends to give preference to the second, because of its scriptural references.

However, from the earliest generations of his disciples, beginning with Ṣadr al-Dīn Qūnawī (who, incidentally, was the first to use the expression *waḥdat al-wujūd*), we see the appearance of treatises which, faithful to the Shaykh al-Akbar's teachings, express them more abstractly, thus making them even more accessible to Western minds. The long introduction that Dāwūd Qayṣarī (d. 1350) gives to his priceless commentary on the *Fuṣūṣ* is quite characteristic in this regard. In the commentary, the teaching of the 'unicity of Being' is so schematically laid out that it allows the reader to understand the way the concepts fit together. At the same time Qayṣarī's schema tends to 'freeze' the teaching into a closed system. This tendency to systematise is quite marked in a number of Persian interpreters of Ibn ʿArabī's teaching whose intellectual formation is based on theological debate and on the school of Avicenna. Notwithstanding the above, it is still preferable to be prudent and to follow the example of these interpreters when setting out reference points for readers who are not familiar with the method of Ibn ʿArabī.

The Unicity of Being

Both Muslim and Christian thought were confronted by the same fundamental metaphysical problem, the one that was raised in the thirteenth century by Albert the Great (who died in 1280 and was thus a contemporary of Ibn ʿArabī): *Utrum esse dicitur de Deo et suis creaturis univoce?* Does the word 'being' have the same meaning when it is applied to God as when it is applied to the creatures, or should we have in mind two different meanings linked by an analogous relationship that constitutes an intermediate status between what is univocal and what is equivocal? The traditional conception of Ibn ʿArabī's thought as the doctrine of 'unicity of Being' clearly indicates that Ibn ʿArabī's answer to this question will be different from that of say Thomas Aquinas, or for that matter, from that of Muslim theologians.

'Being' (*wujūd*) and 'quiddity' (*māhiyya*) are two different concepts. 'Horse' as a concept does not necessarily imply the existence or the non-existence of the horse. But the 'existing beings' (*al-mawjūdāt*) are not such by virtue of a 'being' associated with their quiddity. If quiddity does not possess being, then quiddity is nothing and cannot be associated with anything. If quiddity possesses being, then being cannot be added to it. But if, mentally, we take away being from quiddity, then quiddity is again nothing: thus, being cannot in any way be considered as an accident of quiddity, even if we admit that we are dealing with accidents that differ from, say, whiteness or sphericalness. Nothing can be before or outside of *wujūd*, a univocal word that applies equally to God and to a piece of wood. Quiddity—that by which a thing is such-and-such a thing—is no more than a determiner, or rather an auto-determination, of Being. Its reality, which is purely negative, is that of a limit.

In other words, that which defines a particular thing is the privation from Being that pertains to it, and by reason of which it is a horse, a flower, or a man, and not pure Being; or, to state it another way, by reason of which it is not God. It follows that, seen as an autonomous entity distinct from Absolute Being, the universe is chimerical, since it has no being of its own. It is in this sense that Ibn ʿArabī states, "The universe is an illusion, it has no real existence, as is the case with what is imaginary. In other words, you imagine that it is something different from God, subsisting all by itself, whereas this is not the case at all."[2] On the other hand, if we look at it from the point of view of its relationship to the Absolute Being, of which it is an infinite series of auto-determinations, the universe is totally real.

However, Ibn ʿArabī has no fear of *also* asserting, in apparent contradiction with what has preceded, that "existence in its entirety is reality", or that "there is nothing illusory in existence".[3] A number of passages in the *Futūḥāt* echo this inherent, bilateral dimension of the universe, "The universe is neither pure Being nor pure nothingness. It is total magic: it makes you think that it is God and it is not God; it makes you think that it is creation and it is not creation, for in every respect it is neither this nor that;"[4] "Regarding the realities of the universe, one cannot say that they are God nor that they are other than Him;"[5] "If you say [regarding the universe] that it is real, you are speaking

[2] *Fuṣūṣ*, I, p. 103.
[3] *Mawāqiʿ al-nujūm*, Cairo, 1965, p. 74, and *Fut.*, III, p. 68.
[4] *Fut.*, IV, p. 151.
[5] *Fut.*, III, p. 419.

truthfully; if you say that it is illusory, you are not lying;"[6] "Everything we perceive is the Being of God in the essences of the possible. From the point of view of ipseity, it is His Being; from the point of view of the diversity of forms, it is the essences of the possible [...] In respect to the unicity of its existence [...], it is God, for He is the One, the Unique; in respect to the multiplicity of its forms, it is the universe."[7] The expression *waḥdat al-wujūd*, 'unicity of Being', which is used to refer commonly to the ensemble of the Shaykh al-Akbar's metaphysical teachings seems, in the light of these phrases, to faithfully reflect his thought.

Nevertheless, even if *waḥdat al-wujūd* outlines the main principle that underlies his cosmogony—that there is no being but the Being of God, unique in Himself, but multiple in the forms of His manifestation—it also dangerously reduces this principle by severing it from another principle which is equally fundamental to Ibn ʿArabī's thought. A superficial—or ill-intentioned—reading of these texts and a number of others of similar tenor may lead to the conclusion that if 'God is the being of things', it necessarily follows that 'things are God', that 'everything is God', including dogs, tables, waste bins, and so on. This conclusion, which is pervasive in the writings of Ibn ʿArabī's adversaries, is as simplistic as it is erroneous. It is noteworthy that in the *Wujūd al-Ḥaqq*, a work in which Nābulusī (d. 1731), one of the great representatives of Ibn ʿArabī's school in Ottoman times, responds to Ibn ʿArabī's adversaries, he is careful from the very outset to make clear that "things are not God" even though "He is *wujūd*". The declaration is repeated a number of times, as is the assertion of the neces-

6 *Fut.*, III, p. 275 and II, p. 438.
7 *Fuṣūṣ* I, pp. 101-103.

sary distinction between the Being of God and the 'existing beings'. Ibn ᶜArabī is not saying anything else when he declares, "He is Himself, and things are things",[8] or "The Real is the Real, the creature is the creature (*al-Ḥaqqū ḥaqqun wa'l-khalqu khalqun*)."[9]

The 'Eternal Exemplars' and Divine Knowledge

'Existing beings' are not God and cannot be confused with Him, for they are the 'possibles'; "Know that the universe is all that is 'other than God' and it is nothing other than the 'possibles,' whether they exist or not [...] The status of 'possible' is inherent in them *whether they are existentiated or not;* it is their ontological status."[10] The 'possibles' are neither pure nothingness—which is that which cannot be—nor pure Being—which is that which cannot not be; they are between the one and the other *from all eternity* and *for all eternity.* "From eternity without beginning and for eternity without end, pure possibility can, on the one hand, receive existence and , on the other hand, receive nothingness. Pure Being is God and nothing else. Pure nothingness is that which cannot be and nothing else. Pure possibility is the universe and nothing else; its [ontological] degree is between pure Being and pure nothingness; that which, in it, is turned toward nothingness receives nothingness, that which, in it, is turned toward Being receives existence."[11] The 'possibles' are equally inclined to be existentiated or not to be existentiated; it is the Divine *fiat* that orients their propensity toward existentiation.

But since 'existing beings' possess the status of 'possi-

[8] *Fut.*, II, p. 484.
[9] *Fut.*, II, p. 371.
[10] *Fut.*, III, p. 443.
[11] *Fut.*, II, p. 426.

ble' prior to their existentiation, this implies that they are present, as 'non-existentiated possibles', when the Existentiating Command that makes them manifest on the cosmic plane is given. These 'non-existentiated possibles' to whom the existentiating Word is addressed are the 'immutable entities' (*aᶜyān thābita*), or, to borrow from Meister Eckhart, the 'eternal exemplars'. As Ibn ᶜArabī emphasises, had we not been present to God, we would not have been able to hear the "Be!" that was necessarily addressed to whatever possessed the capacity of hearing.[12] This does not in any way mean that the 'possible' are co-eternal with God, but that they are eternally known by Him, present in His knowledge. God *is* from all eternity; He thus knows from all eternity, and, consequently, He knows the universe from all eternity. "The knowledge that God has of Himself is identical to the knowledge He has of the universe, for the universe is eternally known by Him, even when it is non-existent. On the other hand, the universe, at that moment, does not know itself because it does not exist [...] He never ceases to be and, consequently, His knowledge never ceases to be; and His knowledge of Himself is His knowledge of the universe; thus, He never ceases knowing the universe. Consequently, He knows the universe in its state of non-existence: *He existentiated it according to what it was in His knowledge.*"[13]

The idea of *thubūt*, 'immutability', that is, the mode of presence of the possible in the divine knowledge, has as a corollary the idea of 'predisposition' (*istiᶜdād*). God, since He knows the 'immutable entities', knows their predisposi-

[12] On this subject, cf. *Fut.*, I, p. 168; II, p. 484; III, p. 257.
[13] *Fut.*, I. p. 90.

tions, what they are called to be by their very essence, and He existentiates them according to what they should be. "What you were in the state of *thubūt* is nothing other than what you are in the state of existence, if indeed one can speak of existence with regard to you!"[14] "'Possibles', to the extent that they are distinct, are the manifestation of God in the *loci* that are the 'entities' of the possible, according to the predisposition that is appropriate for these possibles."[15] In order to avoid any confusion regarding the question of 'essences' and 'predispositions' let us bear in mind that the positivity that language attributes to them should not deceive us; properly speaking, 'essences' and 'predispositions' are limits, since what constitutes such-and-such an 'exiting being', as distinct from others and which makes of it a singular occurrence, is *a lack of being.* Its identity is thus defined in the same way that the shadow that surrounds a lighted surface defines its form and its reach; it is its singular share of nothingness.

Metaphysically, the thorny problem of free will that has perpetually tormented theologians in both Islam and Christianity does not even arise here: God wants only what He knows should be. That is what Amīr ʿAbd al-Qādir reminds us of in this passage from his *Book of Stations*, "In everything His act and His choice are according to what the essence of that thing demands. In fact, the universal predispositions are not extrinsic to the things. His acts are determined by His knowledge and His knowledge, in its turn, is determined by its object."[16] Thus, God will respond

[14] *Fuṣūṣ*, I, p. 83.

[15] *Fut.*, II, p. 160.

[16] M. Chodkiewicz, *The Spiritual Writings of Amir ʿAbd al-Kader*, Albany, SUNY Press, 1995, p. 119.

to those who complain on the Day of Judgement that they only sinned through His by saying, "I manifested you in existence in accordance with the knowledge that you gave Me of your essences."[17]

"He does not cease being and you do not cease not being"

Contemplated by God, known by Him, the 'immutable entities' do not know themselves. God knows that they are, but they do not know that He is, nor do they know that they are. In no way synonymous with existence, *thubūt* thus constitutes a 'relative non-existence' (*ʿadam iḍāfī*);[18] present to God, the 'immutable entities' are absent from one another.[19] It is the Existentiating Word that, in manifesting them *ad extra*, provides them with their own individual consciousness. From that point on, they know that they are, "The 'possible' does not know itself until *after* being existentiated by the *fiat*; it is then that it discovers itself, that it knows and that it contemplates its entity."[20] But, and this point is paramount in Ibn ʿArabī's ontological teaching, the 'immutable entities' do not, for all that, acquire 'existence' which the ontological status of 'possible' forbids to them: they are only "dressed" in it.[21] The 'entities of the possible' pass from a 'relative non-existence' (*ʿadam iḍafī*) to a borrowed, and thus 'relative' existence.[22]

This is why Ibn ʿArabī states that the 'possibles' never leave *thubūt*,[23] in other words, they never possess existence

[17] *Fut.*, IV, p. 72.
[18] *Fut.*, II., p. 281 and 587.
[19] *Fut.*, III. p. 254.
[20] *Fut.*, III, p. 254.
[21] *Fut.*, III, p. 47.
[22] *Fut.*, III, p. 193.
[23] *Fut.*, IV, p. 312.

in the strict sense of the word. "Being belongs to Him and non-existence belongs to you; He does not cease being and you do not cease not being."[24] "Know that God alone is qualified by being, and none of the possibles are. Moreover, I say that God is existence itself (*ᶜayn al-wujūd*). "This is what is meant by the *ḥadīth*, 'God is [as Ibn ᶜArabī says, *kāna,* which is generally translated by 'was', has the grammatical value of being present] and nothing is with Him.' By that, he [the Prophet] meant, 'God is (*Allāh mawjūd*) and no thing is.'"'[25] More abruptly, he affirms in the *Fuṣūṣ* that the possibles "never smell the perfume of existence".[26] Manifested *ad extra*, the possibles do not acquire existence; as he insists, they only acquire the ability to be places of manifestation (*maẓāhir*) of Real Being, to the extent of their essential predisposition.[27]

[24] *Fut.*, II, p. 54.
[25] *Fut.*, III, p. 429.
[26] *Fuṣūṣ*, I, p. 76.
[27] *Fut.*, II, p. 484.

"Wherever you turn, there is the Face of God"

I WAS A hidden treasure and I loved to be known: so I created the creatures and made Myself known to them. Thus, they knew Me through Myself." The Shaykh al-Akbar comments frequently on these 'divine words' (*ḥadīth qudsī*), whose authenticity is so often denied by the jurists. According to his interpretation, cosmogenesis is rooted in God's desire to reveal Himself. Wishing to spread His Light, He pulls the 'possibles' out of the darkness of the absolute ignorance, that is nothingness, and propels them into the sun of His Being, so that they may contemplate Him and that He may contemplate Himself in them.

As regards the absolutely simple and unconditioned Divine Essence, "God is independent of the worlds."[1] He is sufficient unto Himself and has no need of His creation. Nevertheless, the author of the *Futūḥāt* remarks that, Divinity (*ulūhiyya*)—in other words, God to the extent that He includes *ad intra* the determinations that are his Names or Attributes—necessarily has need of a *ma'lūh*, of an object upon which His status as Divinity may be exercised. "God, from the point of view of His Essence

[1] Qur'ān 3:97.

and His Being, is 'independent of the worlds'. However, as much as He is 'Lord', He undoubtedly needs vassals."[2] "The Real Being, from the point of view of His Unicity and His Essence, is not what one calls 'God' or 'Lord', since from this point of view nothing can be assigned to Him. That which one calls 'Lord' is in need of a vassal. Than which one calls 'God' needs an object upon which Its divinity may be exercised."[3]

Faithful to the Shaykh al-Akbar's thought, Amir ʿAbd al-Qādir also declares that, "Without God, the creatures would not be existentiated ... and without the creature, God would not be manifested ... Know however that God, in order to manifest Himself by His Essence to His Essence, has no need of creatures, since with relation to Essence, He is absolutely 'independent of the worlds' and even with respect to His own Names ... On the other hand, when He manifests Himself with His Names and His Attributes—which implies the manifestation of the effects—He needs the creatures."[4]

In the same way that His immanence leaves His transcendence intact and vice versa, these two aspects of the Unique Being, God independent of the worlds and God bound up with creation, are eternally concomitant and compatible by reason of the 'concurrence of opposites' that He claims for Himself " He is the First and the Last, the Apparent and the Hidden."[5] The two aspects correspond to the two ontological degrees that Ibn ʿArabī refers to respectively as the 'Absolute Unicity', that of the unconditioned Essence, and the 'Unicity of Multiplicity', that of the Divinity which

[2] *Fut.*, III, p. 364.
[3] *Fut.*, I, p. 328.
[4] Chodkiewicz, *Spiritual Writings*, p. 114.
[5] Qur'ān 57:3.

includes the Names. The passage from *exclusive* unity, which, to avoid ambiguity, would undoubtedly be better referred to as 'unitude', to *inclusive* unity, which implies an internal differentiation, that of the Names, is referred to by Ibn ᶜArabī as '*al-fayḍ al-aqdas*', 'most holy effusion' (what Meister Eckart calls *bullitio*).

The Assembly of Divine Names

The Names are not the Essence, and yet they are no more than He who is designated by them. "At one and the same time, each Divine Name denotes the Essence and the particular meaning that the Name conveys and to which it lays claim. In as far as it refers to the Essence, it includes all the other Names, but in as far as it refers to the meaning that is specific to it, it distinguishes itself from the other Names [...] The Name is thus the Named in respect to the Essence, it is something other than the Named in respect to the particular meaning that it conveys." [6] The plurality of Names does not change the radical simplicity of the Essence any more than creation affects Its eternal solitude. Denuded of everything, the Essence is forever unknown and unknowable. In excluding all multiplicity, it has no knowledge of the creatures, and it has no knowledge of the Names. From this point of view, "God is and nothing is with Him", and the universe is definitely non-existent. This is because the universe draws its existence at every moment from the 'Hidden Treasure' that wishes to reveal its riches, that is, from Being, to the extent that it contains the multiplicity of Names.

The coming into existence of the world is operated by the 'holy effusion' (*al-fayḍ al-muqaddas*) — Meister

[6] *Fuṣūṣ*, I, pp. 79-80.

Eckhart's *ebullitio*. There is little need of specifying that the 'operations' to which we are referring take place in the eternal Divine Present, and that only the structure of human language forces us to describe them as taking place successively over a period of time. The Names, present in the 'inclusive unity', call forth 'epiphanic receptacles' (*maẓāhir*), so that the Names may differentiate themselves in act. "Were it not for the 'possibles', no effect of the Divine Names would have been manifested; and the name is identical to the named, particularly when it is a question of the Divine Names." [7]

On a number of occasions (in the *ᶜAnqā'*, in the *Inshā' al-dawā'ir*, and again in the *Futūḥāt*), Ibn ᶜArabī describes the divine drama that ultimately concludes with the external manifestation of the internal multiplicity of unity. "The Names gathered together in the presence of the Named; they contemplated their realities and their own meanings and they requested that they manifest their effects, so that their entities may be distinguished, the one from the other ..." [8] A cosmic sigh was to resolve this intra-divine tension symbolised by the loving desire of the 'Hidden Treasure' to be known by the presence of the 'Gathering of Names'. The 'exhalation', or the 'breath of the All-Merciful' (*nafas al-raḥmān*, an expression borrowed from the Prophet), produced the 'Cloud' (*al-ᶜamā'*), which Ibn ᶜArabī also calls—borrowing the wording from the Andalusian Sufi Ibn Barrajān—'the reality from which every thing is created', meaning the *materia prima*.

Known by God from all eternity, the 'possibles' thus appear distinctively in the 'Cloud'. Present to God, they are

[7] *Fut.*, III, p. 317.
[8] *Fut.*, I, p. 323.

absent from themselves up to the point when the resounding "Be!" projects them outwardly. "The Breath has its origin in the love that the Divine has for creatures to whom He wanted to make Himself known, so that they may know Him. It is for this reason that the Cloud called 'the reality from which all things are created' appeared. This Cloud is the Substance of the cosmos, and it receives all the forms, the spirits, the compounds of the universe; it is an infinite receptacle. When we were immutable entities in the substance of the Cloud and heard His word 'Be!', we could not do other than come into existence."[9] Ibn ʿArabī remarks that, just as human breath produces phonemes, the Breath of the Merciful generates *kalimāt*, words whose sum constitutes the universe, "The universe is nothing more than His words."[10] We are letters and He is the meaning.[11]

Creation is doubly an act of *futuwwa*, of divine generosity, in respect to the Names and in respect to the creatures. When the 'possibles' are endowed with existence, the Names are able to exercise their authority (*ḥukm*); the request of the Names having been satisfied, the 'possibles' are able to know one another and to know God. Ibn ʿArabī goes on to insist that the Names are our subsistence just as we are theirs. And what are the Names, if not the Named? "Given that the universe does not subsist except through God, and given that the divine attribute does not subsist except through the universe, each one is the subsistence of the other and each one is maintained by the other ..."[12]

Like other spiritual masters, be they Muslim or not, Ibn ʿArabī resorts to the use of diverse metaphors to express this

[9] *Fut.*, II, p. 331; see also pp. 123, 310, and 399.
[10] *Fut.*, I, p. 366; see also II, pp. 390, 395, and 459.
[11] *Fut.*, III, p. 148.
[12] *Fut.*, III, p. 363.

subtle relationship between *ḥaqq* and *khalq*, between God and His creation: the metaphor of light, whose rays are visible only when there is an object to reflect it, that of shadow, which, likewise, is not actually manifest unless it is projected on a surface. The Names are the shadow of God, the rays of His Essence. The creatures are the receptacles that reflect them on a greater or lesser scale according to their own configuration, that is, according to their essential predisposition. Just as the rays are neither the sun nor anything other than the sun, the Names are not God, but they are nothing other than the Named. It may thus be said that the universe "is nothing other than His names", [13] or that "it is the shadow of God", [14] or that "it is nothing other than His epiphanisation in the forms of the immutable entities which cannot exist without it [the epiphanisation]". [15]

Loci for the epiphany of Being, the creatures are similar to the forms that are reflected in a mirror, real and visible to the naked eye, yet absolutely chimerical: if the person in front of the mirror steps away, the image vanishes into nothingness. The same is true for 'existing beings'. At the very moment that one of them appears in existence, its ontological nature as a 'possible' pulls it back into nothingness; devoid of being, it is condemned by its nature to non-being. It is the incessant and perpetually new theophanies that, at each moment, clothe it with a new existence. "'No, in truth they are in confusion regarding the re-creation (*khalq jadīd*)' [16]: the entity of each existing being is renewed at each and every instant; it cannot be otherwise, since God never ceases being the Agent of the existence of

[13] *Fut.*, III, p. 405.
[14] *Fuṣūṣ*, I, p. 101.
[15] *Fuṣūṣ*, I. p. 81.
[16] Qur'ān, 50:15.

the possible."[17] "At each instant, the cosmos, from the point of view of its form, undergoes a new creation, in which there is no repetition."[18] The instant something ceases being is the same instant that God clothes it with another existence, one which is similar but not identical to its preceding existence. Thus, to our limited vision, the universe appears to possess a continuous existence.

"The heart of My believing servant contains Me"

"He who does not contemplate the theophanies with his heart denies them."[19] Like blinding flashes of lightning, these intangible theophanies are seen only with the eye of the heart—the spiritual heart, that is, about which Ibn ʿArabī said, "Know that the heart is a polished mirror, a totally incorruptible surface."[20] A *ḥadīth qudsī* dear to the hearts of Muslim spiritual adepts affirms, "My heavens and My earth do not contain me, but the heart of My believing servant contains Me." The heart of the Perfect Man is so clear that He is able to contemplate Himself in it, so vast that He resides therein, this heart is both the organ of spiritual knowledge and the dwelling place of God. However, just as the elements can corrode metal, the ego and the passions generated by it inflict upon the heart a slow, but certain, death. The heart now becomes inert and insensitive to the incessant flow of theophanies that never ceases, not even for a portion of a second, to shine upon it. There is but one way, one path to regenerate the heart and restore it to its original transparence: the death of this powerful illusion that is called the ego. Let us at this point recall the *ḥadīth* about

[17] *Fut.*, IV, p. 320.
[18] *Fut.*, II, p. 667.
[19] *Fut.*, I, p. 289.
[20] *Fut.*, I, p. 91.

'heroes' who had broken their 'idols', "He whom I love, I am the eye with which he sees ..." Ibn ʿArabī states that the individual who sees through God, sees God through God.[21] Once his heart is purified of the accretions of the carnal soul, "the gnostic possesses a permanent vision of the theophanies; for him, epiphanisation never ceases".[22]

Though all creatures are the receptacles of God, let it be understood that they are not equally so. It is their essential 'predisposition', which they possess from all eternity, that determines the degree to which they are able, faithfully and fully, to reflect the *Mutajallī*, 'He Who epiphanises Himself'. A *ḥadīth qudsī* says, "I am as My servant perceives Me to be"; Ibn ʿArabī explains that this *ḥadīth* means that just as water necessarily takes on the colour of its container, the theophanies are conditioned by the container that receives them and whose form they take on.[23] It thus follows that each individual knows and recognises only that god that he can contain, the god that Ibn ʿArabī calls the 'God created by beliefs'. "That God created by beliefs is the One whose form the heart contains, it is the One who epiphanises Himself to [the heart] and Whom it knows";[24] "When God manifest Himself to him in this belief, it recognises Him; otherwise, it denies Him."[25]

The gnostic transcends this tragedy of an excluded, denied God. He has fully realised the meaning of the Qur'ānic verse that says, "Wherever you turn, there is the Face of God."[26] He knows, or rather, he sees, that there is

[21] *Fut.*, IV, p. 30.
[22] *Fut.*, II, p. 597.
[23] *Fut.*, II, p. 597; III, p. 161; *Fuṣūṣ*, I, p. 226.
[24] *Fuṣūṣ*, I, p. 121.
[25] *Fuṣūṣ*, I, p. 113.
[26] Qur'ān 2:115.

nothing in the universe that is not a place of epiphany. "All sensible and intelligible forms are His places of manifestation." [27] Consequently, there is nothing that does not have its foundation in the divine: "There is nothing manifested in the world that is not based in the divine"; [28] "'Divine support' consists of the fact that the Names are the 'supports' of the places of manifestation in which they exercise their effects." [29] This 'support', which is no other than the Name that, at that moment, 'governs' the creature, constitutes the 'particular face' of every thing, its 'essential reality': "Every reality in the world is a sign that orients us toward a divine reality, which is the basis of its existence and the place of its return;" [30] "There is nothing that is devoid of one of His faces, may He be exalted! He is the reality of that face." [31] This is where idolatry comes from; everything, be it in the sensible or in the intelligible world, is capable of being an object of adoration by reason of the Divine Face that it possesses and which is the very thing that is adored in it. Thus, Ibn ᶜArabī declares that, "God possesses a face in everything that is worshipped;"[32] and "God is that which is worshipped in everything that is worshipped."[33] No matter what religion people follow, Ibn ᶜArabī maintains, they never worship anything but God, whether they know it or not.

[27] *Fut.*, II, p. 661.
[28] *Fut.*, II, p. 508.
[29] Fut., II, p. 654.
[30] *Kitāb al-ᶜabādila*, Cairo, 1969, p. 42.
[31] *Fut.*, II, p. 299.
[32] *Fuṣūṣ*, I, p. 72.
[33] *Fut.*, III, p. 353.

My heart has become capable of all forms
A prairie for the gazelles, a convent for monks,
A temple for idols, a Kaᶜba for the pilgrim,
The Tablets of the Torah, the Book of the Qur'ān.
I profess the religion of Love, and regardless of
which direction
Its steed may lead, Love is my Religion and my Faith.[34]

Care, however, must be exercised. Regardless of what both Ibn ᶜArabī's detractors, and some of his admirers may think, the ecumenism affirmed in this famous poem is not an invitation to combine ideas. Nothing is more foreign to the author of the *Futūḥāt* than the syncretism, of which New Age literature is the most recent manifestation. If spiritual individuals, of whichever religion, perceive a manifestation of the universal Truth in every belief, they nevertheless firmly adhere to their own Law.[35] Though this Law states that, "Your Lord has decreed (*qaḍā*) that you should adore no one but Him",[36] it also prescribes a specific form of worship to which the believers must strictly conform.

Contrary to some interpretations, the decree mentioned in this verse in not only prescriptive (one which can eventually be disobeyed); it is, rather, a question of an irrefutable status imposed upon all creatures. No one can escape from it. Ibn ᶜArabī concludes that all human beings, including those who claim disbelief and including idolaters, in fact worship God, for such is His indefeasible will.[37] After all is said and done, all beings are thus bound

[34] *Tarjumān al-ashwāq*, Beirut, 1966, pp. 42-43; cf. Corbin, *Creative Imagination*, p. 135.
[35] *Fuṣūṣ*, I. p. 196.
[36] Qur'ān 17:23.
[37] On this subject, see *Fut.*, I, p. 405; IV, p. 106; and *Fuṣūṣ*, I, p. 108.

to the Divine Mercy from which, through the 'breath of the All-Merciful', they received existence.

"My Mercy embraces all things"

Another fundamental scriptural reference to be considered is the Qur'ānic verse where God says, "My Mercy embraces all things."[38] Once more basing himself on the sacred text—and on that *literal* reading of the Qur'ān that always guides Ibn ᶜArabī's scriptural interpretations—the Shaykh al-Akbar elaborates a doctrine of apocatastasis[39] (it may be interesting to compare this doctrine to that of John Scotus Eriugena who was, like Ibn ᶜArabī, accused of pantheism). Ibn ᶜArabī maintains that the declaration, "O My servants who have transgressed against themselves, do not despair of God's Mercy; for in truth, God pardons all sins,"[40] is not susceptible to abrogation; and, contrary to the opinion of a number of Qur'ānic commentators, it is not irreconcilable with the verses that affirm the eternity that the damned will spend in hell.[41] He says elsewhere that God has certainly informed us that He will fill Paradise and Hell and that, for some, the stay in hell will be eternal. "But there is no scriptural text relative to the eternity of punishment *to the extent that it is suffering*."[42]

The 'people of Hell', those who, in contrast to sinning believers for whom there will only be a temporary stay, are condemned to remain in Hell will, in fact, never leave it.

[38] Qur'ān 7:156.
[39] Of New Testament origin (Acts 3:21), this word is used to refer to the teaching according to which all creatures will be returned to a state of beatitude at the end of time, thus excluding an eternity of punishment for the damned.
[40] Qur'ān 39:53.
[41] *Fut.*, II, p. 171.
[42] *Fut.*, II, p. 673.

Nevertheless, Ibn ʿArabī maintains that when the time for the sanction expires, instead of producing suffering, punishment will provide a kind of felicity. "Thus, [at the same time] His words 'My Mercy precedes My wrath' [a *ḥadīth qudsī*], His words 'Certainly I shall fill Hell'[43], and His words 'My Mercy embraces everything'[44] will be verified. What I have revealed on this subject, I has not been by personal choice, but because the Divine Word Itself demanded that it be done; I was like someone who was compelled and forced to make a choice."[45] The conclusion that can be drawn from Ibn ʿArabī's doctrine of Divine Mercy that excludes nothing and which does not condemn any creature, no matter how evil, to eternal punishment, is given by Ibn ʿArabī in a conversation between Sahl al-Tustarī (d. 896) and Iblīs, the devil. Iblīs states, "I am one of those things which His Mercy embraces." Ibn ʿArabī comments that, "On this problem, it is Iblīs who was Sahl's teacher."[46]

[43] Qur'ān 7:18.
[44] Qur'ān 7:156.
[45] *Fut.*, II, p. 674; here Ibn ʿArabī points out that the triliteral root of the word *ʿadhāb* (meaning punishment) is *ʿadhb*, which etymologically means 'to be agreeable'.
[46] *Fut.*, II, p. 662.

The Two Horizons

ARABS, KURDS, IRANIANS, and others, all are present at God's appointed time and place. The sanctuary at Mecca is not only a place of prayer and recollection, it is also a meeting place where a multitude of languages, cultures, and ethnic groups come face to face. Like many other pilgrims, the Shaykh al-Akbar made the most of his stay in Mecca by enriching his knowledge and deepening his study of *ḥadīth*. Two years would pass by before he decided to continue his journey. During this extended stay, Ibn ʿArabī produced some new works, and started writing the *Futūḥāt*. Amongst these works, *The Adornment of the Abdāl*, written on 27 January 1203 for two followers (Ḥabashī being one of them) deals with the four pillars of the *via purgativa*:[1] silence, seclusion, fasting, and night prayer. Does this mean that abstaining from speaking, from spending time with one's peers, from eating and sleeping is sufficient for reaching the rank of the *abdāl*, who belong to the spiritual élite that watch over the universe? As all spiritual masters agree, such practices contribute to the slaying of the 'old man'. Nevertheless, if asceticism of the senses is the *sine qua non* condition of all spiritual meta-

[1] Cf. *supra*, page 19, note 1.

morphosis, it is, Ibn ʿArabī emphasises, only in the silence of the mind, in forgetfulness of the self, in intellectual fasting, in the watchfulness of the heart, that the miracle of palingenesis, the rebirth of the Perfect Man, takes place.

Less than a year after writing the *The Adornment of the Abdāl*, Ibn ʿArabī composed the *Rūḥ al-quds*, the *Epistle on the Spirit of Sainthood*, the work which, as mentioned earlier, deals with the sainthood or, more precisely, the *simplicity* of his Western masters. Then, in 1204, he wrote *The Crown of Letters* (*Tāj al-rasā'il*), eight letters in rhymed prose addressed to the Kaʿba whose nobility he was celebrating. To these works, written one after the other, as well as to those which he had begun in the West but finished in the East, should be added the *Tarjumān al-ashwāq* (*The Interpreter of Desires*). Granted, the poems that make up this thin volume were composed much later, at the end of the year 1214. But it was in 1202, in the shadow of the Kaʿba, that the poet began the song of love in which he allowed all the passion that was then consuming him to spill out freely.

Regardless of what those who see him as nothing more than a 'grammarian of the esoteric', Ibn ʿArabī is also—or, more precisely, is first and foremost—a spiritual master devoured by love. The passion for God had already taken complete possession of him many years earlier. But that night, while the Divine Mystery was manifesting itself to him in the person of a Persian girl named Niẓām, the desire that burned within him burst forth in verse. There is no need to specify here that the courtly, even sensual, love that flows through each verse of the *Tarjumān* is no more than the expression, symbolically presented, of the ineffable and the unbearable desire for God. The encounter that Ibn ʿArabī descibes in the prologue to the *Tarjumān* was, of course, with a being made of flesh and blood; a woman whose physical grace and nobility of soul he had no hesitation to describe. Nevertheless, as Corbin so well illustrates in *Creative Imagination*, it was the face of Divine Wisdom that the Shaykh was contemplating and venerating in Niẓām. Clearly, no one is forced to believe this; and when faced with the malevolent insinuations of a few belligerent jurists, the Shaykh felt obliged to compose a detailed commentary on the work, as proof of the purity of his intentions.

The *Tarjumān* was translated into English by Nicholson in 1911; more recently, two partial translations into French have been published.[2] The *Tarjumān* has been quite popular in the West, due in part to Corbin's work. This enthusiasm is wholly justified, for the *Tarjumān* is one of the masterpieces of classical Arabic poetry. The work, however, represents only a tiny fraction of Ibn ʿArabī's poetic output. The greater part of Ibn ʿArabī's poetry, is divided among numerous collections and is to be found in the manuscript collections of several public and private libraries. This *corpus* has yet to be explored. The dispersion of Ibn ʿArabī's poems in the different manuscripts is undoubtedly the result of the conditions that accompanied their composition; the result of a vagrant inspiration, his verses sprang forth with concern for neither time nor place. Ibn ʿArabī did attempt to mitigate the effects of this dispersion by gathering the totality of his poetic production into one work, *The Collection of Divine Knowledge*. Unfortunately there is no complete manuscript of the work extant today.[3]

While still in his youth, in the West, Ibn ʿArabī discov-

[2] *Le Chant de l'ardent désir*, trans. by Sami-Ali, Paris, Sindbad, 1989.

[3] On this subject, see C. Addas, 'A propos du Dīwān al-maʿārif d'Ibn ʿArabī', *Studia Islamica*, Paris, 1995, no. 81, pp. 187-195.

ered that he was a poet. His *Book of the Nocturnal Journey*—as mentioned earlier composed in Fez in 1198—made this abundantly clear. In other words, his calling to poetry took place much earlier than his encounter with the young Iranian woman. It has its roots in a vision that Ibn ʿArabī describes in the long and rich preface that forms the first part of *The Collection of Divine Knowledge*, "The reason I was called to utter poetry (*shiʿr*) is that I saw an angel in dream who brought me a piece of white light; it looked like it came from the sun. 'What is this?' I asked. The answer was 'It is the Sūra *al-Shuʿarā'* ('The Poets').' I swallowed it and felt a hair (*shaʿra*) growing up from my chest into my throat, then into my mouth. It was an animal with a head, tongue, eyes, and lips. It stretched out so far that its head reached the two horizons, that of the East and that of the West. Then it contracted and came back into my chest. I then understood that my words would reach the East and the West. When I came back to myself, I spouted out verses that were preceded by neither reflection nor intellection. From that moment, this inspiration has never ceased."

One does not have to be a scholar of Arabic to notice that the key words in this passage are morphologically related: *shuʿarā'*, 'The Poets', being the title of the chapter of the Qur'ān that Ibn ʿArabī absorbs; *shaʿra*, 'hair', being the product of this communion; and *shiʿr*, 'poetry' being what the vision generates. However, the text is understandable only if it is put together with passages from the *Futūḥāt* where Ibn ʿArabī uses the image of the 'hair' to illustrate the subtle and imperceptible nature of the function of the Muḥammadan Seal,[4] analogous in this regard to the strictly

[4] *Fut.*, I, p. 3, 106; III, p. 514.

initiatory function that Ibn ʿArabī ascribes to 'sacred' poetry.[5] Just as the Seal intervenes in the sphere of sainthood in a veiled way, so must he use allusions and symbols to express himself in order that no impious eyes are able to sully the secret message that he has to offer the *awliyā'*, the 'saints' of the 'two horizons'. Fundamentally ambivalent, poetic language, more than any other form of expression, offers indispensable guarantees of inviolability; only pure souls can successfully decipher the enigmas and symbols which make up its substance.

If nothing else, the vision mentioned above is proof that in Ibn ʿArabī's eyes there is no absolute incompatibility between divine inspiration and poetic inspiration. Of the Qur'ān's 114 Sūras, the fact that it was the twenty-sixth chapter entitled 'The Poets', that gave birth to his poetic work leaves no doubt that it was the Qur'ān itself that nourished his poetry.

Wanderings

The *Rūḥ al-quds* makes it clear that while Ibn ʿArabī resided in the West, he moved exclusively within the circles of Andalusian and Maghreban mystics. He remained resolutely aloof from political life and, although he did occasional have contact with men of letters and *ʿulamā'*, he reserved his teaching for a circle of close friends, followers, and Sufi companions. His mystical investiture in Mecca as 'Seal of Sainthood', however, lead him to give up such marginality. The universal nature of the function that he now effectively assumed, required him to extend his influence beyond Sufi circles, and to attempt to win rulers to his cause.

[5] See C. Addas, 'The Ship of Stone', in J. Mercer (ed.), *The Journey of the Heart*, Muḥyiddin Ibn ʿArabī Society, Oxford, San Francisco, 1996, pp. 5-24.

It is from this perspective that we should view the role of 'advisor to princes' that Ibn ʿArabī played among the Ayyūbids and the Seljuks. The support that several Ayyūbid and Seljuk sultans extended to him, as well as the support that great dynasties—most notably the Ottomans—lavished upon his spiritual heirs contributed to the propagation of his teachings throughout the Muslim world. Nevertheless, if princely support was necessary, it was hardly sufficient. For the 'sacred repository' to reach spiritual adepts of the 'two horizons', Ibn ʿArabī would have to see to it that those who came after him were capable of passing this knowledge on to the future generations.

When he left the Holy Cities in 1204, the Shaykh al-Akbar headed for *bilād al-rūm*, Anatolia, This journey was undoubtedly undertaken at the urging of Majd al-Dīn Rūmī, a high dignitary of the Seljuks with whom he became friends in Mecca. After a stay in Baghdad, followed by one in Mosul, Ibn ʿArabī arrived in Konya in 1205. He was to remain there for just a few months, but, six years later, he was in epistolary contact with Sultan Kaykā'ūs, who had just succeeded his father on the throne. In one brief but famous letter,[6] Ibn ʿArabī, referring to himself as Kaykā'ūs' father, recommended that the sovereign of Anatolia apply the laws that the *Sharīʿa* advocates for Christians in Islamic lands. These recommendations strictly conform to the ideology of Ibn ʿArabī who, in thousands of pages of his work, never ceased to preach strict observance of the Law.

For even though he did recognise the validity of all creeds, and *a fortiori* of all monotheistic traditions, Ibn ʿArabī was nevertheless perennially aware, in those dark days, of the fact that Christianity was becoming a threat to

[6] *Fut.*, IV, p. 547.

Islam on all fronts. In the same year that he penned his letter, the Reconquista in whose shadow he had grown up dealt a fatal blow to the Almohads; on 16 July 1212 the sovereigns of Castille, Navarre, and Aragon united forces and crushed the Muslims at Las Navas de Tolosa. In the East, the third crusade had not only gained the Franks the principality of Antioch and the county of Tripoli, but also the strip of land along the coast from Tyre to Jaffa. The fourth crusade, proclaimed by Innocent III, was to follow shortly thereafter. Granted, it caused little damage to the Muslims, for it was Christians that the *milites Christi* massacred in Constantinople in April 1204, in a blood bath that officially split Christian unity.

The Sultanate of Iconium (Konya) was directly affected by this tragedy that resulted in the splitting of the Eastern Christian empire into three kingdoms: that of the Greeks in Nicea, that of the Comneni in Trebizond, and that of the Franks in Constantinople. The division within the ranks of the enemy was in many ways a blessing for the Seljuks, who made the most of the situation. Masters of a region that had only recently come under Muslim control and where Christians were still in the majority, the Seljuks were obliged to be more vigilant, or at least that was Ibn ʿArabī's judgement.

In 1216, at the end of a long period of wandering through Egypt, Iraq, Palestine and the Hijaz, Ibn ʿArabī returned to Anatolia, where he was to remain for a number of years. The recent death of Majd al-Dīn Rūmī was probably the primary reason for his prolonged stay in Asia Minor. In fact, a number of Arabic and Persian sources report that the Shaykh al-Akbar married Majd al-Dīn's widow and took on the education of his young son Muḥammad, who was later to be known as Ṣadr al-Dīn

Qūnawī (d. 1274). A 'reading certificate'[7] for *The Book of the Theophanies* (*Kitāb al-tajalliyāt*) dated 1230, and thus still during Ibn ʿArabī's lifetime, where Ṣadr al-Dīn is referred to as his son-in-law, confirms the hypothesis of this marriage, which was certainly not the first that Ibn ʿArabī had entered into. Two other wives are mentioned in his writings, one of them being the mother of his son ʿImād al-Dīn, to whom he bequeathed the first draft of the *Futūḥāt*.

The Heirs of the Master

It was his spiritual son, Ṣadr al-Dīn Qūnawī, who some years later inherited the manuscript of the second draft of the *Futūḥāt*. Initiated into the Arabic mystical tradition by his adoptive father, and into the Iranian tradition by Awḥad al-Dīn Kirmānī—a Sufi to whom Ibn ʿArabī had conferred the completion of Ṣadr al-Dīn's education—no one was better placed than Qūnawī to spread Ibn ʿArabī's teachings in those areas under Iranian influence. Strongly influenced by Avicenna's philosophy, well-versed in the dialectic of *kalām* (speculative theology), his writings were filled—contrary to those of Ibn ʿArabī—with the vocabulary and concepts of *falsafa*, philosophy.

Likewise, the differences in accent between the author of the *Futūḥāt* and the author of the *Miftāḥ al-ghayb* (*The Key to the Hidden World*)—Qūnawī's most important work—were considerable. Ibn ʿArabī's writings are to be considered above all as a *testimony*; his doctrinal teaching

[7] The reading certificate (*samāʿ*: 'audition') is an affidavit that appears on a manuscript and is signed by the author of the work. It affirms that the work has been read aloud in his presence and that he has authenticated the text. The certificate usually mentions the date and place of the reading, as well as the name of the reader and the other listeners present.

is inextricably linked to spiritual experience, either his or that of the spiritual masters he knew, and his method, since it defies all rational logic, is often disconcerting. On the other hand, Qūnawī—who, it must be noted, was in correspondence with the great Persian philosopher Nāṣīr al-Dīn al-Tūsī—makes an effort to impart a doctrine. His discussions are precise, ordered, and served by meticulous logic.

Two of his followers emulated his approach: Jandī (d. 1291), who composed a commentary on the *Fuṣūṣ*, and Saᶜd al-Dīn Farghānī (d. 1300), whose commentary on the *Naẓm al-sulūk* (Ibn al-Fāriḍ's great mystical poem) was prefaced by a methodical exposé of Ibn ᶜArabī's metaphysical doctrine. Qāshānī (d. 1329), and then Qaysarī, both also authors of commentaries on the *Fuṣūṣ*, were, in the fourteenth century, the main links in the Iranian school of Ibn ᶜArabī begun by Qūnawī. What all these authors have in common is their concentration on the *Fuṣūṣ*, the most 'abstract' of Ibn ᶜArabī's writings, and the close interpretation of *kalām* and *falsafa* in their lines of argument. In so doing they have not, of course, altered Ibn Arabi's teachings. But, in their desire to organise, they both schematised and impoverished it. Through them, Ibn ᶜArabī's teaching became, on the one hand, more accessible and on the other hand more vulnerable to the criticism of the *ᶜulamā' al-ẓāhir*, in other words the exotericists. However, their writings profoundly influenced all the later development of philosophical and mystical thought in Iran, even within the very core of Shīᶜite gnosis. Corbin's writings in this area have shown the extent to which the works of Ḥaydar Āmulī (d. 1385) and Mūllā Ṣadrā (d. 1640) were indebted to Ibn ᶜArabī's teachings.

But Ibn ᶜArabī's influence on the Indo-Iranian continent went far beyond the boundary of this 'intellectual' current of which we have done no more than mention the most eminent representatives. At the end of the thirteenth century in Iran, a whole poetic tradition, inspired by the Shaykh al-Akbar and in vernacular language, sprang up and has continued down the centuries. Very popular, this literary genre—of which Shabistarī's famous *Rosary of Mystery* is quite representative—was one of the main vectors of the popularisation of Ibn ʿArabī's teaching in the most remote corners for the Muslim world. Fakhr al-Dīn ʿIrāqī (d. 1289), another of Qūnawī's followers, was one of the first representatives of the movement. His poems, especially those in the *Lamaʿāt*, inspired generations of Sufis in the Turco-Persian world. His influence was especially notable on Jāmī (d. 1492). This saint from Herat and author of a great number of works on mysticism, one of which was a commentary on the *Lamaʿāt* and another a commentary on the *Fuṣūṣ,* was one of the chief links in the transmission of Ibn ʿArabī's heritage in the fifteenth century. At the time, Sufism in India was already deeply impregnated by the key ideas of Ibn ʿArabī's teachings, to such an extent that, according to Annemarie Schimmel, "commentaries on the *Fuṣūṣ* and works explicating the theories of the Great Master numbered in the thousands".[8]

Thus Ibn ʿArabī's prolonged stay in Anatolia is of considerable importance given its repercussions for the future of his teachings. However, we should not forget that his repeated trips to Cairo, Damascus, Baghdad, Mosul, and Aleppo also contributed, during his lifetime, to the spread of his teachings in the Arabic world. Ismāʿīl Ibn Sawdakīn, who met the Shaykh al-Akbār in Cairo in 1207, was among

[8] Schimmel, *Mystical Dimensions of Islam*, Chapel Hill, University of North Carolina Press, 1975, p. 357.

his closest followers. Though not numerous, his writings were essentially faithful, and thus priceless, transcriptions of Ibn ʿArabī's oral explanations: rather than comment on his master, he preferred to remain his humble scribe. ʿAfīf al-Dīn Tilimsānī, as his name suggests a native of Tlemcen, met Ibn ʿArabī in Damascus in 1237, having spent time with Qūnawī in Anatolia. The author of a famous *dīwān*, and of a less well-known commentary on the *Fuṣūṣ*, Tilimsānī was to be branded by the doctors of the Law as the "most pernicious" (Ibn Taymiyya was the first to use the word) of Ibn ʿArabī's followers. In addition to Ibn ʿArabī, Tilimsānī had been influenced by another 'heretic', of whom he became both the disciple and the son-in-law: Ibn Sabʿīn (d. 1270). A native of Murcia, the famous author of the *Budd al-ʿārif* (*What the Gnostic Worships*) is well known to students of medieval European history because of his correspondence with Emperor Frederick II, to whom he addressed his famous *Sicilian Replies*. But for Ibn Taymiyya and his cohorts, Ibn Sabʿīn was nothing more than the dangerous protagonist of 'absolute unicity' (*al-waḥda al-muṭlaqa*), a doctrine which, in contrast to Ibn ʿArabī's 'unicity of Being', emphatically asserted that the universe is pure illusion in all respects.

Initiated into the Shaykh al-Akbar's teachings in the Yemen, ʿAbd al-Karīm Jīlī (d. 1408) was certainly one of the most original interpreters of Ibn ʿArabī's doctrine. The author of *The Perfect Man* (*al-Insān al-kāmil*) did not hesitate to disagree with Ibn ʿArabī on some points; what he had in common with him was the connection between doctrinal teaching and personal spiritual experience. Nābulusī was less audacious and more methodical than Jīlī. He wrote a number of treatises aimed at clarifying and defending Ibn ʿArabī's teaching, which explains the often apologetic tone of his works. It was finally in the western part of the Muslim world, in nineteenth-century Algeria, that Ibn ᶜArabī's tradition became fully resurgent in the person of Amīr Abd al-Qādir. Elevated to the status of a national hero after Algeria's independence, this famous adversary of the French was actually a great 'Akbarī' master. His work, *The Books of Stations*, for a long time unknown in the West, testifies to this.[9]

Aside from this scholarly literature, the technical language of which significantly limits the number of its readers, there emerged very early on another, more accessible genre which quickly spread Ibn ᶜArabī's teaching well beyond the circle of *litterati*. The works of Shaᶜrānī (d. 1565), who paraphrased Ibn ᶜArabī rather than commented on him, played an important role in this respect; a number of later Arabic language authors who referred to the Shaykh al-Akbar's teachings knew these teachings only second-hand, having learned them through the writings of this prolific Egyptian. In order for this list to be comprehensive, we must include the numerous writers who, contrary to those mentioned above, did not openly claim to be followers of Ibn ᶜArabī—and sometimes even refuted his teachings—but whose poetic or prose works were tributaries of his thought and conveyed, whether they wanted them to or not, both his most important ideas and his vocabulary.

Ibn ᶜArabī was thirty-eight lunar years old when he arrived in Mecca. About the year 1221, at the age of around fifty-eight, he buried Ḥabashī in Malatya and his second son, Saᶜd al-Dīn, was born. A final long period of wandering now began and proved to be, from a literary point of view, particularly fertile. Travelling where fate led him, Ibn

[9] See the partial translation by M. Chodkiewicz in *Spiritual Writings*.

ᶜArabī continued to compose a multitude of works. Many of these are short treatises only a few folios long, but two books are especially deserving of attention: *The Book of Theophanies* (*Kitāb al-tajalliyāt*), whose 109 chapters highlight the esoteric meaning of the verses of the second Sūra of the Qur'ān; and *The Revelations of Mosul* (*al-Tanazzulāt al-mawṣiliyya*), where he gives a mystical interpretation for the ritual prayer and its gestures.

The countless reading certificates signed by the Shaykh during these twenty years are evidence that his oral teaching intensified. Examination of these priceless documents shows an increase in the number of his followers, or, to be more precise, the emergence of a group of 'sympathisers'. For the most part, the newcomers who were not necessarily from Sufi circles, resided in the places where the reading sessions took place, these newcomers were not necessarily from Sufi circles. It can also be seen that the number of audience members varied, depending on the tone of the work in question. Writings that were, from a doctrinal point of view, more 'neutral', like the *Rūḥ al-quds*, understandably attracted larger audiences; conversely, readings of his more hermetic treatises, like the *Tāj al-rasāᶜil*, tended to be reserved for a small circle of initiates. Though eager to open his teaching to a wider public, Ibn ᶜArabī was nevertheless aware of the need to observe the discipline of secrecy in some areas.

About the same time as Ibn ᶜArabī's final wanderings, a number of events were confirming the inevitable dissolution of *dār al-islām*. The Ayyūbid regime was floundering among fratricidal struggles, and the fifth crusade was being organised. Off to free the Holy Sepulchre, the crusaders laid siege to Damietta in February 1218. Sultan Kāmil, who was head of the Ayyūbid confederation at the time, was not in the least reluctant to offer Jerusalem, Ascalon, Tiberias to his enemies; in short, all of his uncle Saladin's prestigious conquests, in exchange for the crusaders' withdrawal. But Pelagius, the Pope's prelate, remained steadfast, and on 6 November 1219, Damietta fell into his hands. Will we ever manage to find out what Saint Francis of Assisi felt about this event? According to a number of medieval Christian accounts, he was present at the time. We can at least be sure that the *Poverello* had quite a different conception of the mission of 'Christian chivalry' (see box).

How Saint Francis converted the Sultan of Babylon to the faith

Saint Francis, driven by his zeal for the faith of Christ and his desire for martyrdom, once crossed the sea with twelve of his most saintly companions, in order to come face to face with the Sultan of Babylon. They arrived in a Saracen country where the roads were guarded by men who were so cruel that no Christian who passed by ever managed to escape death. As it pleased God, they were not killed, but taken, beaten, and bound, then led before the Sultan. And in his presence, Saint Francis, inspired by the Holy Spirit, preached faith in Christ so divinely that, in order to prove it, he even asked to be allowed to walk through fire. The Sultan became greatly devoted to him, as much for the constancy of his faith as for the disdain for the world that he saw in him—for, even though poor, he would accept no gifts—and for the fervour he continued to see in him for martyrdom. From that time on, the Sultan willingly listened to him, and begged him to come back to see him often, and he generously allowed him and his companions to preach wherever they wished.

From *Les Fioretti de Saint François*, pp. 101-102

"Benefit from my existence"

"GO TO SYRIA," the Prophet had said, "for it is the purest of God's lands, and those who live there are the élite from among His creatures." Partially occupied by the Franks, threatened by the Turks, the *bilād al-shām*, the 'land of Syria', aroused covetousness from all sides. Damascus, particularly, was the stake and the victim of rivalries between Ayyūbid princes who attempted, each in turn, to take possession of it. Despite all this, it was Syria—rather than Egypt, to which the majority of Maghrebans had emigrated—that Ibn ᶜArabī chose as his second homeland. He must certainly have been aware of the many words attributed to the Prophet that sang the country's praises. However, this does not preclude the possibility that more pragmatic considerations played a role in his decision. For it happened that, over the years, the Shaykh al-Akbar had won the sympathy of powerful individuals in the course of his numerous stays in Damascus. One prominent family, the Banū Zakī, who for generations had held the position of administrative judge (*qāḍī*), provided him with lodgings and saw to his needs. Nor was this an isolated case. An examination of sources, written by the Shaykh al-Akbar and by others, shows that Ibn ᶜArabī had friendly relations with the most eminent doctors of the Syrian Law, some of whom gave him alms on a daily basis.

Whatever the reasons, Ibn ʿArabī chose to settle in Damascus in 1223. He was above sixty years old, and the time had come to put an end to his earthly wanderings. Called the 'Sanctuary of the Prophets'—according to local traditions, some seventy thousand of them had been laid to rest there—Damascus held particular status in Islam's eschatological topography. It is Damascus that, at the end of time, will welcome the Son of Mary when he returns to earth to complete the cycle of creation. For the time being, the 'fiancée of cities', offered asylum to the Shaykh who, at the end of an active life, was able to enjoy a peaceful but studious old age.

"Benefit from my existence before I leave", the Shaykh declared to his companions one day.[1] Time was of the essence, and Ibn ʿArabī was well aware of this. He dedicated his remaining years to writing and to his disciples. In 1234, he had barely completed the first draft of the *Futūḥāt* when he began the second draft. Simultaneously, he was continuing his work on his poetic *summa*, the *Collection of Divine Knowledge* (*Dīwān al-maʿārif*). Besides these works, which are colossal in their own right, he composed a number of other books—twenty-five, according to Osman Yahia's estimation[2]—among which was the *Fuṣūṣ*. Few of his followers were aware of the *Fuṣūṣ*, the work which, as we have seen, crystallised the polemics around him.

Prudent rather than guarded, Ibn ʿArabī took the greatest of precautions when divulging his esoteric teachings. Works like the *Fuṣūṣ* and the *ʿAnqā' al-mughrib*—let alone those which dealt with the science of letters—were the

[1] *Fut.*, I, p. 723.
[2] Yahia, *Histoire et Classification de l'Oeuvre d'Ibn Arabi*, Damascus, IFEAD, 1964, I, pp. 106-107.

object of reading sessions behind closed doors, sessions which were rarely attended by more than two or three of his disciples. Had he acted otherwise, Ibn ʿArabī would probably have met the same fate as his contemporary al-Ḥarrālī who, accused of heresy, was thrown out of Damascus in 1235. Let us not forget that the Syrian metropolis was at the time the spearhead of Sunnism in the East. Those who were religious, be they *ʿulamā'* or Sufis, did not hesitate to publicly denounce the policies of Ayyūbid sovereigns, whom they accused of conspiring with the enemy. Empassioned speeches on the duty for *jihād* were put into action by the likes of Shaykh al-Yūnīnī, who was given the title 'the Lion of Syria' and who participated in all the battles against the

The 'Lion of Syria' and the Virgin Mary

He [Shaykh al Yūnīnī] was sitting in his *zāwiya* one day when a woman appeared leading a horse loaded with fabrics and copper articles. She tied her horse, approached the shaykh, and greeted him. "Who are you?" he asked. "A Christian from Jubbat al-Qunayṭra [on Mount Lebanon]." "What brings you to my house?" "I saw Our Lady Mary in a dream, and she said, 'Go and put yourself in the service of Shaykh Abd Allāh al-Yūnīnī until you die.' I said to her, 'O Mistress, he is a Muslim!' 'So? He is of course a Muslim, but his heart is Christian.'" The shaykh said to her, "Mary is the only one who knows me!" The shaykh gave her lodging in his *zāwiya* and she remained in his service for eight months, and then she fell ill. The shaykh asked her, "What do you wish?" "I wish to die in the religion of Mary." The shaykh sent for a priest to come [...] and she died with him.

Abū Shāma, *Tarājim*, 617AH
From *Les Fioretti de Saint François*, pp. 101-102

Franks. There was, however, no fanatism in this fiery combattant of the faith who, without the slightest hesitation, agreed to shelter a Christian woman who had come to beg asylum in the name of the Virgin Mary (see box).

The Letter and the Law

It is hardly surprising that, in such a climate, the return of Jerusalem in 1229 caused a fierce reaction. In all likelihood, Ibn ʿArabī's voice joined those of the Damascene protestors who denounced the treaty of Jaffa concluded between Sultan Kāmil and Emperor Frederick II. A Muslim sovereign handing over the third holiest city of Islam to the enemy could only have raised the Shaykh al-Akbar's indignation. In a passage of the *Futūḥāt*, where he supports his argument with a number of scriptural references, he leaves no doubt about his opinion on the subject. Ibn ʿArabī categorically states that it is illicit to go to Jerusalem or to live there as long as the city is under enemy control.[3] This is proof, if proof be needed, that Ibn ʿArabī's ecumenism was strictly subordinate to respect of the Law; the Law which prescribes indulgence and generosity in some cases, while in others—especially when it comes to maintaining the territorial integrity of *dār al-islām*—it calls for firmness and rigour. God alone is the infallible judge, and there is no fairer judgement than His.

In this manner, the Shaykh invites his reader to conform rigorously and in each circumstance to the edicts of the Divine Law, to the exclusion of every other personal consideration.[4] "He who holds to his Lord's prescriptions is the 'hero';"[5] "The 'hero' [let it be borne in mind that for Ibn

[3] *Fut.*, IV, p. 460.
[4] *Fut.*, I, p. 242; IV, p. 13.
[5] *Fut.*, I, p. 242.

ʿArabī this word refers to the spiritual élite] is he who is in the hands of canonical knowledge like a corpse is in the hands of the washer of the dead;"[6] "The happy man is he who conforms to divine prescriptions and does not transgress them."[7] And the author of the *Futūḥāt* rises up against the Bāṭiniyya who, maintaining that they know the hidden meaning, claim to be exempt from observance of the Law. They are, he says, "the most ignorant of men in the field of subtle truths."[8] It must be admitted that all these statements are clear evidence against the permissiveness (*ibāḥa*) directed at Ibn ʿArabī by his detractors. Some orientalists, it is true, have shown their belief in this thesis by presenting the Sufis in general, and Ibn ʿArabī in particular, as Islam's 'outlaws' *stricto sensu* of the word: pure theosophists who have reached beatitude to be liberated from the shackles of Qur'ānic law. Such an interpretation, when applied to Ibn ʿArabī, does not stand up to even a moderately attentive reading of his work.

"Revealed Law is identical to essential reality [...] the Law *is* essential reality."[9] For the *Doctor Maximus*, there is no antagonism between *Sharīʿa* and *ḥaqīqa*, between Sacred Law and the eternal truths of which the law is both the sign and the vector. As we have seen, all his teachings tend to show that man can only restore his original theomorphism by fully accepting his ontological servitude. It is thus by submitting body and soul to this Law which, at every instant, claims his servitude that he can rise from "the lowest of the low"[10] to the primordial dignity of "the most

[6] *Fut.*, II, p. 233.
[7] *Fut.*, IV, p. 28.
[8] *Fut.*, III, p. 273; I, p. 334.
[9] *Fut.*, II, p. 562-563.
[10] Qur'ān 95:5.

perfect stature".[11] "The entire Law constitutes the spiritual states of the *malāmiyya*."[12] It is not possible to illustrate more clearly that the highest sainthood, the same sainthood that Ibn ᶜArabī assigns to the 'people of blame', is nothing more than obedience to the Divine Commandments: a blind—in the literal sense of the word—obedience, just like the obedience of the 'eternal exemplars'.

The orthodoxy preached and practised by Ibn ᶜArabī was probably the cause of the respectful regard that the Syrian *ᶜulamā'* accorded him during his lifetime. However, Ibn Ḥajar al-Asqalānī (d. 1449) was quite right when he attributed the *ᶜulamā*'s benevolence to the fact that they did not have a sufficient understanding of his teachings. Most likely, they would have shown themselves much less understanding if they had been aware of his theses regarding jurisprudence (*fiqh*). This is an issue of paramount importance, since it concerned not only mystics, but the entire Muslim community. In a sense, it was the social order that was in question; one might even wonder if that was not the real motive behind the persecutions that have pursued Ibn ᶜArabī for the past seven centuries.

The Qur'ān, and then the *ḥadith*, are the two scriptural sources of Islamic jurisprudence. The 'way of reading' the Holy Book consequently plays a fundamental role in the interpretation of the Law and in the way the Law is applied. In an earlier chapter, we saw that Ibn ᶜArabī places great emphasis on the *form* of divine discourse. "It is not in vain," he says, "that God discards one word in preference for another."[13] The occurrence, but also the absence or repeti-

[11] Qur'ān 95:4.
[12] *Fut.*, III, p. 36.
[13] *Fut.*, IV, p. 67.

tion, of a word, even the simplest of particles, cannot be called fortuitous when it is the Eternal Who is expressing Himself. Uncreated, the Divine Word is not a support for the Truth, it *is* the Truth; it is both the signifier *and* the signified. The hidden (*bāṭin*) meaning is consequently to be found nowhere else but in the apparent (*ẓāhir*) meaning. This way of reading might be considered literal; but it is not at all unequivocal. The more it adheres to the sacred text, the richer the exegesis is in interpretations, provided nothing is excluded from what divine grammar includes. Thus, the boldest of the theses of Ibn ᶜArabī's teachings, those of apocatastasis and universality of faith, emerge from this rigorous faithfulness to the Letter.

This decidedly literal interpretation equally guides Ibn ᶜArabī's legal thinking, "Everything about which the Law remains silent has no legal status other than its original licitness."[14] God is not absent-minded; His silences are not omissions. It is not for man to fill in the 'voids' in Revelation. Here, we have a veiled criticism of the tendency of jurists to inordinately increase the constraints imposed upon the faithful, when their role should be to facilitate, as much as possible, the observance of the divine commandments. At the same time, Ibn ᶜArabī is condemning the partisan quarrels of the doctors of the Law who forbid the believer to adopt an easier interpretation of the sacred law when it is sanctioned by a school other than their own.[15] The jurist has no more right to fill in the 'gaps' in Divine Law than he has to compensate for its 'ambiguities'. As soon as the Divine Law leaves the field open to a number of solutions, none of these, and certainly not the easiest, has a right to be discarded, "God imposes upon a soul only that

[14] *Fut.*, II, p. 165.

[15] *Fut.*, I, p. 392.

which it can bear";[16] Divine Law is strict, but it is not rigid.

In the voluminous chapters of the *Futūḥāt* that Ibn ʿArabī devoted to questions of jurisprudence, concern for lightening the burden of legal obligations shows up time after time. But in no case should he be seen as espousing laxism of any kind: Ibn Arabi—and this cannot be repeated often enough—would not tolerate any transgression of the Law. And if, to those who interpreted the Law for the 'mass of believers' he recommended leniency, for himself and for those who wanted to follow in his footsteps he would not permit recourse to facilitating solutions, even completely legitimate ones.[17]

Mercy towards others, steadfast rigour towards himself: these are the defining poles of Ibn ʿArabī's ethics. This should not come as a surprise, for the Seal of Muḥammadan Sainthood, the supreme heir to him who was sent "to all men"[18] "as a mercy for the worlds"[19], could bring no other message than that of universal mercy. Since he was 'made' to preserve the 'sacred repository', his role was also to remind spiritual individuals of 'both horizons' that the Perfect Man is he whose absolute adherence to the Law and to the Letter has led him back to his origin when, present to God, he was absent to himself.

[16] Qur'ān 2:286.
[17] *Fut.*, I, p. 723.
[18] Qur'ān 34:28.
[19] Qur'ān 21:107.

Opinions of Ibn ᶜArabī

THE ORIENTALISTS

Louis Massignon (*Essai sur les origines du lexique technique de la mystique musulmane*):

"Ibn ᶜArabī, through decisive and irremediable concessions, hands Muslim mystical theology over to the synchretic monism of the Qaramita. It is not only souls, but all of creation that he presents as emanating from God, following a cosmogonic evolution in five stages [...] and, as for mystical union, it is through an inverse movement, of ideal involution in five stages, that, summing up all of creation in our thought, 'we re-become God'."

"This synchretic eclecticism keeps [Ibn ᶜArabī and 'certain pseudo-mystics'] from perceiving the irreparable transforming differentiation that, along the way, gradually takes place between those who prostrate themselves along the 'Way of the Cross' and those who lay down under Juggernaut's cart."

Henri Corbin (*Creative Imagination in the Sufism of Ibn ᶜArabī*):

"... a spiritual genius who was not only one of the greatest masters of Sufism in Islam, but also one of the greatest mystics of all time [...] Genius of the complexity of Ibn ᶜArabī's, as radically foreign to religion of the letter and of dogma as it is to the schemas that such religion facilitates, has sometimes been branded with the word 'synchretism'. This is the insidious, lazy explanation of the dogmatic mind that is alarmed when it encounters operations of thought that fail to obey the imperatives of its interior norm and which, personally, is no less rigorous. To be content with such an explanation is to admit one's own failure, one's own powerlessness to even get a sense of this norm which cannot be reduced to any school of thought or any collective conformism."

MUSLIM AUTHORS

Ibn Taymiyya (d. 1328) (*Letter to Shaykh Manbijī*):
"At first, I was one of those who had a favourable opinion of Ibn ʿArabī and respected him because of the worthwhile things I had read in his books, like what he says in a number of passages of the *Futūḥāt*, in the *Kunh*, in the *[Amr] al-muḥkam al-marbūṭ*, in the *Durra al-fākhira*, in the *Mawāqiʿ al-nujūm*, etc. I had not yet perceived his true aim and I had not yet read the *Fuṣūṣ* and other similar writings [...] When the matter had become clear, I realised what my true duty was."

Ibn Khaldūn (d. 1382) (*fatwā* in response to a question about the *Fuṣūṣ al-ḥikam*):
"Regarding the legal status of books that contain pernicious beliefs and copies of them that have been disseminated among people, like Ibn ʿArabī's *Fuṣūṣ* and his *Futūḥāt* [...] [this is followed by a list of works by other authors], the rule about these works and others like them is that they should be destroyed wherever they are found, either by burning them or by erasing with water any trace of writing on them. The reason for this is the general advantage that comes from obliterating pernicious beliefs and from their disappearance, lest they lead those who read such books astray."

Al-Aḥdal (d. 1451) (*Kashf al-ghiṭā'*):
"The theses of this Ibn ʿArabī and his likes are patent disbeliefs. He and his followers are among the worst of infidels, heretics, and profligates [...] Since their misbelief is deviant, whoever agrees with their doctrine, approves of it, or affirms—as they, themselves, maintain—that it does not deviate from religion is both a disbeliever and an apostate."

Amīr ʿAbd al-Qādir (*Kitāb al-mawāqif*):
"It is through the Shaykh al-Akbar that was sealed the Sainthood identified with Muḥammad's heritage. In fact, he was one of the "solitary ones" (*afrād*) to whom belong the degree of free and general [not law-giving] prophethood, and to this he added the possession of the Muḥammadan heritage that was sealed by him."

Chronological table of Ibn ʿArabī's life

DATE	BIOGRAPHICAL EVENTS	HISTORICAL EVENTS
1163		The construction of Nôtre-Dame of Paris began
1165	Birth of Ibn ʿArabī in Murcia	
1167		Birth of Gengis Khan
1172	His family settles in Seville	
1180		Start of the reign of Philip Augustus
1182		Birth of Saint Francis of Assisi
1187		Saladin captures Jerusalem
1190	Vision of all the prophets in Cordoba	Death of Christian of Troyes
1193	Ibn ʿArabī crosses the Strait of Gibraltar for the first time to go to Tunis	Death of Saladin
1194	Return to Seville; death of his father writes the *Book of Contemplations*	Birth of Frederick II
1195	Ibn ʿArabī marries off his two sisters in Fez, then returns to Seville	Victory of the Almohads at Alarcos
1196	Second sojourn in Fez	
1198	Writes the *Book of the Nocturnal Journey* in March; attends the funeral of Averroes in Cordoba in December	Innocent III becomes Pope
1199	Writes the *Setting of the Stars* in Almeria	Death of Richard the Lion-Heart

1200	Ibn ʿArabī leaves Andalusia permanently	
1201	Last sojourn in Tunis; departure for the East	
1202	Arrives in Mecca; encounter with the *fatā*; starts writing the *Futūhāt*	
1204	Ibn ʿArabī leaves Mecca to travel around the East	Fourth Crusade; sack of Constantinople
1212	Epistle to the Sultan of Anatolia	Defeat of the Almohads at Las Navas de Tolosa
1214	Writes the *Tarjumān al-ashwāq*	
1215		Gengis Khan takes Peking; Frederick II becomes emperor
1216	Ibn ʿArabī moves to Anatolia for a few years	
1219		Fifth Crusade; The Franks take Damietta; Saint Francis of Assisi goes to Egypt
1223	Settles permanently in Syria	
1225		Birth of St Thomas Aquinas
1226		Start of the reign of Saint-Louis; death of Saint Francis of Assisi
1227		Death of Gengis Khan; excommunication of Frederick II
1229	Vision of the Prophet from whom he receives the *Fuṣūṣ*	The Sultan Kāmil hands over Jerusalem to Frederick II
1231	Completes the first draft of the *Futūḥāt*	
1233		Start of the Inquisition
1236		Fall of Cordoba
1238	Completes the second draft of the *Futūḥāt* on 3 November	
1240	Death of the Shaykh al-Akbar on 8 November	

Bibliography

Addas, C., 'A propos du Dīwān al-maᶜārif d'Ibn ᶜArabī', *Studia Islamica*, Paris, no. 81, 1995, pp. 187-195.

Addas, C., *Quest for the Red Sulphur. The Life of Ibn ᶜArabī*, Cambridge, The Islamic Texts Society, 1993; originally published as *Ibn Arabī ou la Quête du Soufre Rouge*, Paris, Gallimard, 1989.

Addas, C., 'The Ship of Stone', in J. Mercer (ed.) *The Journey of the Heart*, Muḥyiddin Ibn ᶜArabī Society, Oxford, San Francisco, 1996, pp. 5-24.

Asín Palacios, M., *L'Islam Christianisé. Études sur le Soufisme d'Ibn Arabī*, Paris, Guy Trédaniel, 1982.

Atlagh, R., 'Paradoxes d'un Mausolée', in *Lieux d'Islam. Cultes et Cultures de l'Afrique à Java*, Paris, Autrement, 1996.

Austin, R. W. J. (trans.), *Sufis of Andalusia. The Rūḥ al-quds and al-Durrat al-fākhirah of Ibn ᶜArabī*, London, 1971; French trans. by G. Leconte, *Les Soufis d'Andalousie*, 3rd edn, Paris, Albin Michel, 1995.

Beaurecueil, S. (de), 'Mémoire de l'homme ou mémoire de Dieu', in MIDEO, 22, 1994, pp. 73-94.

Chittick, W.C., *The Sufi Path of Knowledge*, Albany, SUNY Press, 1989.

Chittick, W. C., *Imaginal Worlds: Ibn al-ᶜArabī and the Problem of Religious Diversity*, Albany, SUNY Press, 1994.

Chodkiewicz, M., *The Seal of the Saints: Prophethood and Sainthood in the Doctrine of Ibn ᶜArabī*, Cambridge, The Islamic Texts Society, 1993; originally published as *Le Sceau des saints. Prophétie et sainteté dans la doctrine d'Ibn Arabī*, Paris, Gallimard, 1986.

Chodkiewicz, M., *An Ocean without Shores*, Albany, SUNY Press, 1995 .

Chodkiewicz, M., *The Spiritual Writings of Amir ᶜAbd al-Kader*, Albany, SUNY Press, 1995.

Chodkiewicz, M. *et al.*, *Les Illuminations de la Mecque. Textes Choisis/The Meccan Illuminations. Selected Texts*, Paris, Sindbad, 1988.

Corbin, H., *Creative Imagination in the Sufism of Ibn ᶜArabī*, Princeton, Princeton University Press, 1969.

—*Spiritual Body and Celestial Earth*, Princeton, Princeton University Press, 1977.

Dhahabī, Shams al-Dīn, *Mīzān al-iᶜtidāl,* 3 vols., Beirut, 1963.

Hirtenstein S. and Tiernan M. (eds), *Muhiddīn Ibn Arabī: A Commemorative Volume*, Shaftesbury, 1993.

Ibn Shaᶜār, *ᶜUqūd al-jumān*, in *al-Dirāsāt al-islāmiyya*, vol. 26, 1991.

Izutsu, T., *Unicité de l'existence et création perpétuelle en mystique islamique*, Paris, Les Deux Océans, 1980.

Izutsu, T., *Sufism and Taoism*, Tokyo, Iwanami Shoten, 1983.

Les Fioretti de Saint François, Paris, Éd. du Seuil, 1994.

Massignon, L., *Essai sur les origines du lexique tecnique de la mystique musulmane*, Paris, Librairie Philosophique J. Vrin, 1968.

Schimmel, A., *Mystical Dimensions of Islam*, Chapel Hill, University of North Carolina Press, 1975.

Sivan E., *L'Islam et la Croisade*, Paris, Adrien Maison-

neuve, 1968.
Yahia, O., *Histoire et classification de l'oeuvre d'Ibn Arabī*, 2 vols., Damascus, IFEAD, 1964.

WORKS BY IBN ᶜARABĪ INCLUDING TRANSLATIONS

Dīwān, Būlāq, 1855.
Dīwān al-maᶜārif, ms, B. N. 2346.
Kitāb al-ᶜabādila, Cairo, 1969.
Fuṣūṣ al-ḥikam, ed. ᶜAfīfī, Beirut, 1946.
Futūḥāt al-makkiyya, Cairo, 1329 AH.
Kitāb al-tajalliyāt, Tehran, 1988,
Kitāb wasā'il al-sā'il, M. Profitlich (ed.), Freiburg, 1973.
Mawāqiᶜ al-nujūm, Cairo, 1965.
Rūḥ al-Quds, Damascus, 1970.
Tarjumān al-ashwāq, Beirut, 1966.
Las Contemplaciones de los Misterios (*K. Mashāhid al-asrār al-qudsiyya*), ed. of Arabic text and Spanish trans. by S. Hakīm and P. Beneito, Murcia, 1994.
Les Dévoilement des effets du voyage (*K. al-isfār an natā'ij al-asfār*), transl. by D. Gril, Combas, Éd. de l'Eclat, 1994.
Les Illuminations de la Mecque (*al-Futūhāt al-Makkiyya*). Translated extracts: Chapter 167, *L'Alchimie du bonheur parfait*, trans. S. Ruspoli, Paris, Berg International, 1981; Chapter 178, *Le Traité de l'amour*, trans. M. Gloton, Paris, Albin Michel, 1986; Chapter 367, *Le Voyage spirituel*, trans. M. Giannini, Louvain-la-Neuve, Bruylant-Academia, 1995.
L'Interprète des Désirs Ardents (*Tarjumān al-ashwāq*), full English trans. R.A. Nicholson, London, 1911; 1978 (2nd edn); partial French trans. Sami-Ali, *Le Chant de l'Ardent Désir*, Paris, Sindbad, 1989.

Le Livre de l'arbre et des quatres oiseaux (*Risālat al-ittihād al-kawnī*), trans. D. Grill, Paris, Les Deux Océans, 1984.

Le Livre de l'extinction dans la contemplation (*K. al-fanā fī al-mushāhada*), trans. Michel Vâlsan, Paris, Les Éditions de l'Oeuvre, 1984.

Le Livre d'enseignement par le formules indicatives des gens inspirés (*K. al-iᶜlām bi ishārāt ahl al-ilhām*), trans. Michel Vâlsan, Paris, Les Éditions de l'Oeuvre, 1983.

La Niche des lumières (*Mishkāt al-anwār*), trans. Muhammad Vâlsan, Paris, Les Éditions de l'Oeuvre, 1983.

La Parure des abdāl (*K. hilyat al-abdāl*), trans. by Michel Vâlsan, Paris, Les Editions de l'Oeuvre, 1992.

La Sagesse des prophètes (*Fusūs al-ḥikam*), partial trans. by T. Burckardt, Paris, 1955; English trans. T.J.W. Austin, *The Bezels of Wisdom*, New York, 1980.

La Vie merveilleuse de Dhū-l-Nūn al-Misrī (*al-Kawkab al-durrī fī manāqib Dhi l-Nūn al-Misrī*), trans. R. Deladrière, Paris, Sindbad, 1988; Paris, Albin Michel, 1995 (2nd edn).